Cowboy Boots

Cowboy Boots

Written by Tyler Beard

Photographs by Jim Arndt

Gibbs Smith, Publisher

This book is dedicated to the cow.

First Edition

12 11 10   10 9 8 7 6 5

Text © 2004 Tyler Beard
Photographs © 2004 Jim Arndt

Published by
Gibbs Smith, Publisher
P.O. Box 667
Layton, Utah 84041

Orders: 1.800.748.5439
www.gibbs-smith.com

Cover design by Kurt Wahlner
Book design by Modern Grafik

Printed and bound in Korea

Library of Congress Control Number: 2004108299
ISBN 10 : 1-58685-522-0
ISBN 13 : 978-1-58685-522-2

Contents

Heel to Toe 8

Well-Heeled and Sassy 30

Women in Boots 46

From the Hide 70

Over the Tops 80

Stars and Stripes 86

Boot Garden 92

Skulls, Bones, Cactus and Critters 128

Toolin' Around 140

Saddle Up 168

Things That Fly 196

Tantalizing Toes 226

The Height in Fashion 240

Heart and Sole 250

Boot Camp 310

Boot Anatomy 315

The Bootmakers 316   The Museums 327   The Vintage Dealers 328

The pair that started it all . . .

Acknowledgments

First and foremost I want to thank all the bootmakers, past and present.

Bootfuls of kisses, hugs, respect, appreciation, and thank-yous go out to: Betty Jo and William Claud, for sticking me in "the pair that started it all" ★ Big Sis ★ Dr. A. and Dr. G. ★ Patti, for offering ★ Friend and kindred spirit Madge Baird ★ Kurt, for your boundless energy ★ Donna Foster, for your time, patience, and happy face ★ Honorary "bootist" Jennifer June ★ Jim Arndt—boot authority, collector, and camera man par excellence ★ Diana and Jack Gotcher, my boot godparents and guardians ★ "Boot sister" Wendy Lane ★ My pal, Jack Parsons ★ Caren Clark, for just being you ★ The original "bootists": Jack Pressler, Mark Hooper, Gary van der Meer, John Tongate, and tatterdemalion, boot archeologist, professor of bootology, and the original soul of the cowboy boot—Evan Voyles ★ Butch Brown, the best bounty boot hunter ever! ★ Kathy and Eddie Kimmel ★ Bryce Sunderlin, "stay the course" ★ Scott Emmerich and Jerry Black (Tres Outlaws), who keep raising the bar on boots ★ The collectors: Jeff Borin, Robert Brandis, Sharon and Bryant Dalby, Jon Henderson, Nathalie Kent, Eric Lamalle, Marty Newman, Carolyn Shapiro, Weasel Bob, aka "The Corkster," Bill Welch, Johnny Wright, Evan and Gail Voyles, Claudia Voyles, Sandra and Fausto Yturria ★ Special thanks to all the museums in our resource guide ★ Last, but always first in my heart, my "Squirrel Girl," Teresa Lynn and our furry daughter, Baby Doll, aka "Dotty," who both give me something to look forward to every day.

—*Tyler Beard*

My thanks to:

Tyler "Mr. Cowboy Boot" and Teresa, Madge, Dave, Tony, Scott and Jerry, Corky, Evan, Eric, Jack, Jon, Amado, Curt, Craig, all the bootmakers and collectors, and especially the best-dressed cowgirl Nathalie for her incredible boot designs, and for all her support and love.

—*Jim Arndt*

Olsen-Stelzer, 1940s.

Heel to Toe

*A*fter twenty years of research, it has become clear that there was no "first" pair of cowboy boots. As far back as we know, horsemen through the ages, all over the world, preferred higher-heeled boots. This represented a sign of nobility or a profession on horseback, above the ground, *hence the old term* well heeled.

For millennia, horsemen have relied on protective footwear, including Attila the Hun in the fifth century, the Moors in the eighth, Genghis Khan in the twelfth, the Spanish conquistadors in the sixteenth, and horsemen throughout nineteenth-century Europe and the Americas. Man, his boots, and the horse have been inexorably linked in history, legend, myth, and our imaginations.

Before and after the Civil War, cowboys wore whatever they could afford, or what they walked away from the war in. Early daguerreotype photographs show groups of cowboys wearing a sundry of clothing and footwear.

We know that by 1870 John Cubine, in Coffeyville, Kansas, had combined the Wellington and military-style boots in what is known today as the Coffeyville-style boot. The earliest Coffeyville boot is usually described as not having a specific right or left foot; as being constructed from unlined, waxed, flesh-side-out leather, usually in black; as having leather pull straps, a low Cuban heel, slightly rounded square toes, a fully pegged sole, with the front of the boot, or the "graft," being considerably higher than the back. Not

Left: vintage 1930s; right: 1930s Nocona with Bohlin silver appliqué.

always, but usually, the graft was a different color of leather—brown or a deep dried-blood red. The advent of reverse lathes and lasting techniques gave the Coffeyville-style boot its own left and right foot.

Throughout the 1870s, these various military-style boots were copied in hundreds of variations, modified and sometimes improved upon by the gone-to-Texas southerners, who also took with them the refined, cavalier, European-style ancestry of bootmaking, with its higher heel and finer leathers. During these times, heel shapes and boot heights varied greatly. Toes were usually of round or square duckbill shapes that might be as wide as three inches. Stitching on the boot tops for support or decoration was fairly rare, and wrinkles, toe bugs, or flowers stitched on the toe tops were unheard of.

By the 1880s, a more characteristic cowboy boot was being developed with four-piece construction and a stovepipe top (which means the front and back of the boot were the same height). Some simple decorative stitch patterns were emerging, and the high heel was becoming much more popular. The historical facts show that the most influential bootmakers in Kansas and Texas pre-1900 were primarily of German or British descent. Indisputably, Charles Hyer of Hyer Brothers Boots in Olathe, Kansas, and "Big Daddy Joe" Justin of Justin Boots in Spanish Fort, Texas, were the two most influential bootmakers of the 1880s. The Italian shoe- and boot-making influences of Tony Lama and the Lucchese family weren't felt until after the turn of the century.

By the end of the 1880s, the general public was already nostalgic about the disappearance of the Old West, and by the turn of the century, the cowboy stood alone as the most picturesque and heroic figure in the nation. His profession had changed little since the 1860s. His range, corrals, cattle pens, and cow trails were far from the patted-down town roads and city streets. Cowboys were still out there pounding dirt into dust, mud into muck, and snow into slush. A cowboy's best friends were his horse and saddle, a rope, a hat, and a crackling fire to warm his work-weary feet and dry his indispensable cowboy boots.

Above: Tom Mix vintage boots, 1920s; left: vintage 1940s.

The work, vanity, and whimsy of the cowboy began to have a dramatic effect on the style of the boot. Heels went from low to high, to low, and back to high again. Toes were of varying widths in square and round shapes. Some soles were thick while others were thin, and the tops could be plain, stitched only to help hold them up, or decorated by two colors of leather. The result was a perfect tool for the feet to be used in a very personal way.

One of the decorative whimsies was the toe wrinkle. They may not have been the first to stitch them on boots, but in 1903 the Hyer Brothers were the first to advertise "toe wrinkles"—the straight or curved stitched lines that lay across the top of the foot—in their catalogs. This toe decor was also referred to as a flower, bug, or fleur-de-lis. With the exception of exotic skins, this personalized bootmaker's signature in thread remains an essential element on both mass-manufactured and custom-made boots today.

In the 1920s and '30s, boots rose to a fashion high as a by-product of the entertainment industry's success with cowboy heroes. Western style was kept alive through radio shows and movie serials featuring the likes of Tim McCoy, William S. Hart, Bronco Billy, Jack Hoxie, Buck Jones, Kim Maynard, Hoot Gibson, and working cowboy, stunt man, and movie star with a capital "C" for class, Tom Mix. None of these tough hombres would have been caught dead without their boots on. In fact, these Hollywood idols were the springboard for the fashion vs. function, "anything goes" cowboy boot styles of the next three decades.

Some of these new abstract designs had been devised from popular western icons and nature themes: floral images, vines and leaves, tulips, roses, scrolls, and curlicue stitch patterns were incorporated in ever-increasing colors and variations. Hair-on longhorn heads, spiderwebs, cactus pears, eagles in flight, horses and horseshoes, bucking broncs, oil derricks, card suits, crescent moons surrounded by stars, and endless varieties of butterflies, initials, and brands all but replaced the simpler geometric inlaid boots of the 1920s and 1930s.

Vintage 1955–65.

In the post–World War II years, entertainment was requisite for war-weary Americans. By now, the Wild West Shows were over; similarly, the old-time ranch rodeo became, instead, an organized town and city sporting event. Boots became much more than protection against rattlesnakes, *mesquite thorns, cacti, inclement weather, saddle chafing, or even a means to hold up a pair of working spurs. This was show business. The entertainers in these events realized the need to exaggerate the styles and colors of their costumes in order to be seen from the grandstands. In addition, the dude-ranch-vacation phenomenon had swept the nation. Families hopped into their station wagons or boarded trains for the West in order to dress up and play cowboy and cowgirl. The impact of cowboy crooners such as Gene Autry, Roy Rogers, and Dale Evans, along with the Nashville country music scene, was the key to the mass appeal that put cowboy boots on the feet of people of all ages, in all states, and in all professions.*

The big five—Justin, Tony Lama, Nocona, Hyer, and Acme—began to crank out millions of pairs to satisfy this first wave of national cowboy boot mania.

Looking back, it is impossible not to consider 1940 to 1965 as the Golden Age of bootmaking. This was the time when bootmakers pushed all the limits of their imaginations and skills. During this period, western clothing crossed all gender boundaries more than any decade before or since. Boots were being made in a variety of shapes, colors, styles, and leathers unimaginable only a generation before.

In the mid-1960s, John Wayne was competing with the Beatles for the admiration of the American youth. Western heroes and western style undeniably took a back seat for a while. During this period, boots took on a more conservative appearance; the sharp, narrow box toe and the needle nose were all the rage. Just like the fins of a Cadillac, the boot had streamlined itself. Heels were of a lower, walking style and flat. The bright colors and inlaid designs were no longer popular, nor were short-top peewees. The cowboy boot industry prevailed as an American fashion classic throughout the '60s and into the era of the hippie and the fringed-moccasin boot craze.

The 1970s rolled along with few changes to the cowboy boot. Although most toes were still basically pointed and heels were low, a new trend was on the horizon: the leisure suit and polyester influence had arrived, unfortunately. The tanneries were in a fluster trying to match all those

**Above: vintage 1940s;
right: vintage 1955–65.**

21

Vintage 1955–65.

weird pastels and powdery colors. The state of the cowboy boot had reached an all-time low.

When Urban Cowboy, *starring John Travolta, was released in 1980, the redneck hippie look of the late '70s was suddenly replaced with redneck chic. By 1985, however, as with all trends, the urban cowboy had ridden off into the sunset. The paddle-footed, two-tone pale and pastel boots of the early 1980s were now passé. Two 1985 movies—*Top Gun, *starring Tom Cruise wearing a pair of vintage inlaid boots, and* Silverado, *which was the stepping off point for fashion boots in the entertainment industry—seemed to reignite a genuine interest in classic cowboy styles of the 1890s through the 1960s. It was during this time that anything western, especially cowboy boots, was being sold at a frenetic pace worldwide. The vintage-boot stores in New York and on Melrose Avenue in Los Angeles were going great guns selling nothing but vintage boots and copies of boots from the Golden Age of bootmaking. The retro-cowboy-boot stampede had begun, and the first renaissance of bootmaking was well underway by 1991, finally challenging* *the creativity and artisanship of the Golden Age. The urbane cowboy had arrived.*

In 1992, The Cowboy Boot Book *was released. Boot aficionados now had a bible to study by. Its positive influence on the boot industry sent customers scurrying to their favorite bootmakers to order boots directly designed from, or inspired by, new and old designs featured in the book.*

In that book, I challenged the bootmakers, through words and pictures, to surpass and surprise us all by raising the bar and sending all of us boot wearers into a new Platinum Age of creative bootmaking. They rose to the challenge and reinvented what cowboy boot dreams are made of. Here we go again, Art of the Boot *was released in 1999 as a testament to the true art and boundless collaborations between customer and creator. In that book I responded to the most frequently asked question, "What's new in cowboy boots?" In bootdom at that time, it was the women bootmakers.*

While women have always been a driving force behind many a bootmaker, and a large percentage of boot tops have always been stitched by

Ray Jones, 1960–70.

women, the new thing is the advent of women owning their own shops and making their boots from beginning to end. In this male-dominated profession it seems that the survival of a woman bootmaker is a rare and precious thing.

Nudie's, 1960–70.

The "First Lady" of cowboy-bootmaking, Enid Justin (sister of the Justin brothers; started Nocona Boot Company in 1925), never made a complete pair of boots herself, but she knew as well as any bootmaker how a boot should be made—an important factor when you are the owner and president of one of the top five boot-manufacturing companies in the world. Up until 1980, no women had their own boot shops. Enid died in 1990 at age ninety-six, and if she were still around, she would be very proud of how far women have come in bootmaking. Melody Dawkins has the distinction of being the first woman to own her own boot shop, followed by Deanna McGuffin, Heather Joy, Stephanie Ferguson, and Lisa Sorrell, all superlative bootmakers who are not just surviving but are thriving.

The buzz on boots has never died down. This second renaissance has taken less than a few years and appears to be spurred by a seemingly endless wealth of imagination and talent. More and more, saddle makers and leather crafters are being called upon to carve boot tops of every description: portraits of loved ones and pets, a favorite boat or classic automobile, commemorations of weddings, birthdays, and special events, all beautifully executed, hand-painted and -stained in a rainbow of colors.

Embellishments have gone wild too. Hand beading has popped up. Other additions are artier than ever: multicolored rivets and rhinestones, machine and hand embroidery, pull straps and long mule ears embellished with sterling silver conchos, ornate stitching, and inlays and overlays. The ancient Mexican art of pitiado (the fine art of hand stitching with cactus fiber) makes a prize of a pair of boots, as do an endless parade of gold, ancient coins, diamonds, and precious stones set into boot leather. Cowboy boots now exist in a land of no restraints.

The worldwide popularity of the cowboy boot perennially astounds the high-fashion market and trickles down to the masses. This enduring popularity is partially explained by the fact that cowboy boots conjure up curiosity, conversation, compliments, and contemplation. They have a life of their own. They mesmerize. The cowboy boot is the world's greatest fashion enigma, and a boot silhouette is the most recognized western icon.

Cowboy boots come with plenty of attitude built-in between those layers of luscious leather. They imbue confidence, individuality, sexuality, and bootfuls of good old American moxie with style. They can be as unique and personal as a tattoo, but you can take them off at night. That's the long and short of it, from heel to toe.

Above: Hyer Boots, 1935–45; right: vintage 1950s.

ed and Sassy

The one thing that high-fashion divas have in common with rodeo champs and rodeo queens is that when their feet are boot-shod they rule the runway like it was the open range. Whether deliciously decadent or even decidedly dull, cowboy boots never fail to raise the eyebrows of the opposite sex and the attitude of all. A boots-eye view reveals that although we still have a plentitude of ranches, rodeos, working cowboys and cowgals, most folks today regard their boots as a fashion accessory—not a working necessity.

Step into this kingdom of boots, where variations on a shape are infinte,

Left: vintage 1940s;
right: Hyer Boots 1950–60.

a place where footed pride is a profusion of pump and circumstance, where pretty mingles with practical and the rough roams with the refined. In this fertile land, rampant with feats of fancy, black and brown have befriended and now exchange glances with electric blue, gold, fiery orange, hot pink and lime; fur-lined, feathered, beaded, and baubled boots abound.

Left: Lucchese for Acme, 1940s; above: Charlie Dunn for Capitol Saddlery, 1950s; right, above: vintage 1950s; right: vintage 1940s.

33

Left: Sorrell Custom Boots;
above: Justin Boots, 1950s;
right: vintage 1940s.

Left: vintage 1950–60;
above: Charlie Dunn.

Left: vintage 1950s;
below left: vintage 1930–40;
below right: Lucchese;
right: vintage 1930–50.

Left: Little's Boots;
above: L. White 1955–65.

Little's Boots;
right: Zeferino Rios, 1955–65.

Super Bowl Boots

In the current "Super Bowl of Boots," Dave Wheeler ran with this pair and scored the winning touchdown. There have been many pairs of boots through the decades fashioned from football leather, but nothing like these. Houston executive Warren Savery began his obsessive football odyssey way back in 1981, attending each and every NFL Super Bowl contest. He had no idea that twenty-three years later his fascination with football would artistically pass to his own feet! A winning team was in play when Warren approached Wheeler in March of 2004. After an enthusiastic huddle on the finished design, a shared vision was reached and kick-off time was near. The game plan was to replicate details from spectator tickets, stir in the various cities and sports logos, sprinkle in game dates and football memorabilia—all assembled from ten types of hide in forty-three colors. The crowning touch is the wingtip toes christened by diminutive Lombardi trophies circled by a cluster of hand-laced mini footballs—a booty unsurpassed, sewn up with more than 1,300 hand-tied knots. The total finish time exceeded 300 hours. Result? One unique pair of cowboy boots fashioned with a labor of love, a touchdown and truly one of the "seven wonders of the bootmaking world."

Wheeler Boots.

Paul Bond Boot
Company;
right: Tres Outlaws

men in Boots

Singer and actress Bette Midler once quipped, "Give a girl the correct footwear and she can conquer the world." Shoes aside—boots are boss. Forever a symbol of strength and stamina, boots are for the brave and the bodacious. Boots have won battles in bedrooms, boardrooms, and battlefields of all descriptions. In short, boots bestow confidence. Let's not forgot that Joan of Arc, rabble-rouser and visionary, was brassy and sassy in her thigh-high cuissarde-style leather boots.

We all associate thigh-high boots with the buccaneers. Their boots weren't just a pirate fashion statement. Those guys actually stuffed and stored gold, jewelry, small loot, and smuggled items in their boots for transport and safekeeping. This

Rocketbuster Boots.

practice gave way to the terms bootlegging *and* booty.

It was not until the mid-1800s that nonworking women first ventured out

in a variety of bootish wonders: equestrian riding boots, the galoshed half-boot, and laced ankle boot. These new fashion delicacies were designed to make the foot appear diminished and dainty, sleek and slim. Whether buttoned or laced, the idea was to be all snugged up. A time when the female leg was still being obscured from public view, this attempt to hide and hinder the foot and ankle, in fact, had the opposite effect.

The shape of a woman's leg was no longer a mirage in the mind but engendered further curiosity and fantasy. It didn't take long for these blushing beauties in their booties to feel the empowerment and talismanic spell that their fashionable new feminine footwear possessed. By the 1850s, boot-wear for all women was being mass-produced. The boot became a bolstering and

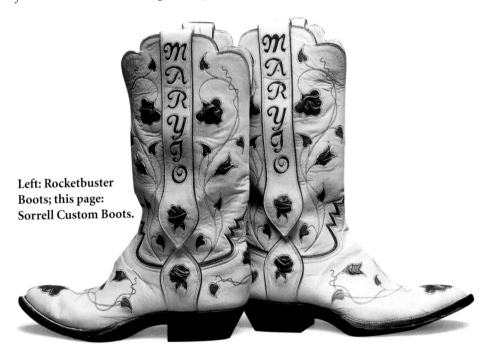

Left: Rocketbuster Boots; this page: Sorrell Custom Boots.

bona fide symbol of the slow-rising equality of the sexes.

The "bicycle boot" was all the rage in the 1890s, crafted in canvas, Moroccan kid, and floral brocades, this high-rising, laced and latticed, pedal-seeking slim-jim was the precursor to the more utilitarian "packer."

Like the cowboy boots of today, the "opera boots" of the 1890s were fast and flashy, flamboyantly designed in velvets, satins, silks, and brocades, then garnished with pearl buttons, metallic embroideries, beads, jewels,

**Above: Liberty Boots;
left: Tres Outlaws.**

and golden tidbits. Sweet and sala-
cious poems to solicit adoration and
enhance flirtation from heel to toe.

But it seemed that in a click of a
heel, boots were out. For fifty years
boots on women were rarely seen
outside of a rodeo arena or sporting activity. Not until the 1960s
did the boot hum become a buzz.
Boots were reborn and the whole
kit and kaboodle came in with a
bang! While true westerners were
still donning traditional calfskin
in twelve-inch cowboy-style tops,
pointed toes and one-and-a-half-
inch heels, the fashion industry had

**Above: Tres Outlaws;
below: Rocketbuster Boots.**

J. P.'s Custom Boots;
right: Rocketbuster Boots.

gone berserk on the boot. The 1950s "Spanish ankle boots" with their stiletto toes pointed the way to the future—the Space Age, in fact, ushered in by white plastic "go-go" boots by Courrèges, in 1964. Widely imitated and wildly varied, these boots were not "just made for walkin."

Boots never mind bragging: they did become the largest-selling footwear worldwide in the 1960s. Topsy-turvy was the order of the day, everything traditional was juxtaposed with the unconventional; it was all "downside up." There was a myriad of ankle boots; "the bootie," "the genie," the convertible," "the zip," "the bootette," "the pixie," "the Beatle," and the taller yet ever-present "Wellie," no longer relegated to green and

Little's Boots.

black but catapulted in a kaleidoscope of primary and psychedelic colors. In 1973, before the skintight leather platform boots from Britain crossed the pond, a store in London named Biba sold more than 75,000 pair in just two months! Although you could punch the sky in this five-inch booster boot, platforms were nothing new. In sixteenth-century Venice, "chopine" shoes elevated women to an unbelievable thirty inches off the ground. At times, two assistants were required for balance and support. (Popular again in the late 1930s and 1940s, and again in the 1990s, it appears that platforms are bound to rise again in a couple of decades, if not sooner.)

Larry Mahan put a woman's fashion high heel on the cowboy boot in the late 1970s, inlaid with multicolored floral pastels with butter, putty, and beige backgrounds. Mahan single-handedly put the "cowboy" back in the boot for women. They were not the genderless shorties or "peewees" of the his-and-her 1940s and '50s, not the "steady boots" or the "rodeo twins," but what goes around always comes around, so hang on. . . .

The 1970s and '80s also embraced the "dingo" and "the ghillie." But when Debra Winger and John Travolta two-stepped their way across Texas in Urban Cowboy *(1980), we were once again reminded that boots really do belong to both sexes. It took five long and glorious years of boot-making madness for the Urban Cowboy craze to squelch itself. However, before the renaissance of custom boot-making we are currently experiencing, and even before the second coming of the "Golden Age" of bootmaking (1989–99), that gap of four years (1985–89) was pretty much a siesta for boots and their makers, a time to reflect and*

Opposite: Paul Bond
Boot Company;
left: J. P.'s Custom
Boots.

reinvent. The only trend during that period was the rebirth of the "shoe boot"—basically the "topless boot." In the 1930s and '40s this little bootless boot was first seen struttin' its stuff on the square-dance floors and honky-tonks across the West—an answer to better ankle movement while dancing. The reviver was Georges Marciano for Guess. As in the first go-round, he made them exactly the same for men and women—some laced, and some slipped on. They could be worn with jeans, skirts or dresses, like a boot, but still not quite a cowboy boot for all occasions.

The 1990s were the anything-goes decade for boots. The custom bootmakers rose to the challenge and created the Platinum Age of western footwear.

So what's new on the high-heeled horizon? The fashion cowboy boot, a hybrid where the New York runways meet the Old West, where heights, heels, hides, and colors have collided head-on with the tried-and-true traditions of western footwear for both men and women.

Vintage 1940s.

William Shanor and Julie Bonney.

James Leddy Boot Company.

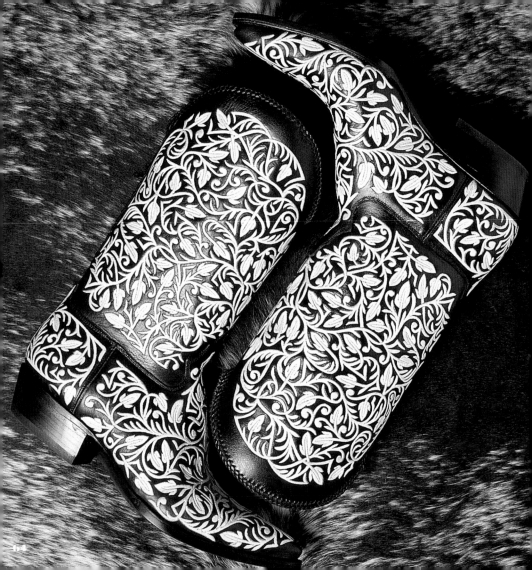

Left: Liberty Boot Company;
this page, clockwise from left: Justin Boots,
1940s; Old Gringo; Justin Boots, 1940s.

65

Opposite,
clockwise from
upper left:
Kimmel Boots,
Tres Outlaws,
Little's Boots,
Tres Outlaws;
this page:
Liberty Boot
Company.

Clockwise from top: vintage
1950–60; Wheeler Boot
Company; vintage 1950–60.

Left: Stephanie Ferguson Custom Boots; below: Liberty Boot Company.

Tres Outlaws;
opposite; Little's Boots.

There is no denying the fact that most people are drawn in by— and, in fact, love—the fragrance of new leather. It is sensuous and primeval; there was a time when just about everything came from a cow or some other critter. Leather "anything" is still considered to be luscious and luxurious.

Cowboy boots are certainly no exception— they are the rule. There is a varied and veritable heaven of hides from tanneries all over the world. Just about anything that walks, slithers, swims, flies, or crawls has at one time been applied to a pair of boots. In tantalizing textures from shiny patents to distressed and patinaed, the color spectrum is so far over the rainbow that hundreds of colors and textures have been customized, plucked from nothing on this earth. Hides are a tactile pleasure; yet, some are chosen simply for their durability: usually a tough skin such as buffalo, horse, mule, ox, shark, stingray, wildebeest, or good-old cowhide is impregnated with oils during the tanning process, adding longevity to its new life as a pair of boots. Ostrich and kangaroo are supple yet rugged, in contrast to their reputation for dress and elegance. French calf is still touted as the Rolls

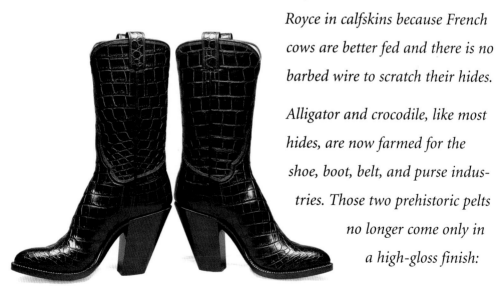

Royce in calfskins because French cows are better fed and there is no barbed wire to scratch their hides.

Alligator and crocodile, like most hides, are now farmed for the shoe, boot, belt, and purse industries. Those two prehistoric pelts no longer come only in a high-gloss finish:

Opposite: Michael Anthony; this page: Tres Outlaws.

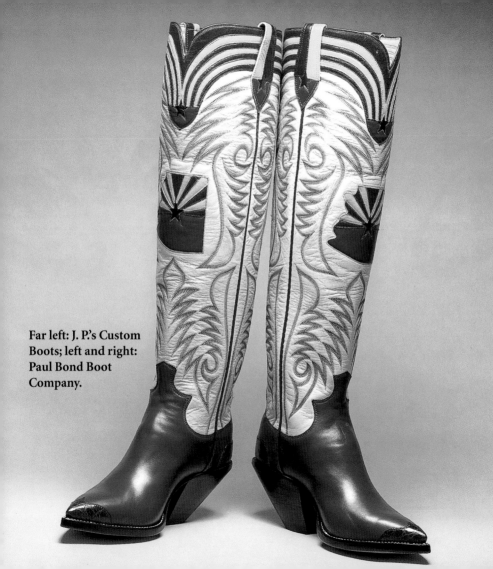

Far left: J. P.'s Custom Boots; left and right: Paul Bond Boot Company.

Above: Rocketbuster Boots; right top: Tres Outlaws; right bottom: Kimmel Boots.

garment gator is soft and sleek, while "oily" gators are more durable and scuff resistant. If you want a furry boot, a feathered boot, or something a little more down home, such as toad, armadillo, deer, or rattlesnake— no problem.

And, although I don't know any bootmakers offering them at this time, Hannibal Lecter be warned, there is a pair of boots (pre-1900) in the Smithsonian made from human hide.

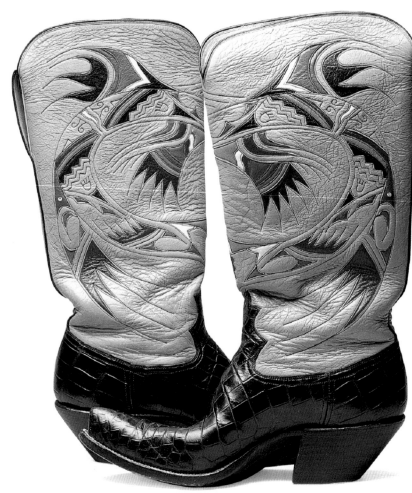

Sorrell
Custom
Boots.

Little's Boots.

Tres Outlaws.

Over the Tops

Those little things that stick up above the top of the boot are the ears, more commonly called "pull straps." They are what you grab onto while you pull the boots on—and sometimes that can be a challenge. A diversity in pull straps exists that ranges from the understated, plaintive, and utilitarian to a pair of doggone, grandiose, full "mule ears," all inlaid and overlaid in a dozen vibrating colors that might spell out the state you reside in on one side and the name of your favorite beau or belle on the other—a pair of gobsmacking lu lu's that start at the top of the boot and end at ground zero.

Cheeky and grabable, mule ears are not for the faint of heart. What you pull your boots up and on with could be likened to customizing the final flourishes on a hot rod. In the early days, the scraps from the boot leather were used, then cotton pin stripes and canvas cloth, all usually sewn to the

Rocketbuster Boots; opposite, left to right: Olsen-Stelzer, 1940s; child's boot, pre-1900; vintage 1930s.

inside of the boots so that working cowboys could avoid catching them on branches, prickly pear, horns, steel, rock, and rope. From the 1930s to the '50s, when men and women frequently tucked their trousers and jeans into their boots, bootmakers, and especially the factories, began a clever marketing technique of stitching their logo name, town, and state on those pulls, which then hung above or flopped over the boot—free advertising with every pair sold.

Both plain pulls and pulls with a punch are easy to come by these days. As with all the other frosting applied to a pair, the boot buffet offers up endless varieties of the sublime, the lighthearted and the ornate, all designed to lend a personal signature to not only what you have on but how you get them on.

Above: Tres Outlaws; right: Rocketbuster Boots.

Hyer Boots, 1962;
opposite: Little's Boots.

and Stripes

"**O**' say can you see" these layered leather paragons of patriotic perfection? If not, you've been blinded by the spangle and sparkle of these spectacular boots. It seems odd that flag boots apparently didn't arrive on the scene until after World War II. The first pair that has been documented is a pair made by The Palace Boot Shop that appeared in Life *magazine.*

Flags on the feet are usually resigned to the stars and bars, the red, white, and blues and the stately eagle glistening boldly in gold, or simple "streamer" stripes that almost everybody likes. I can't help but

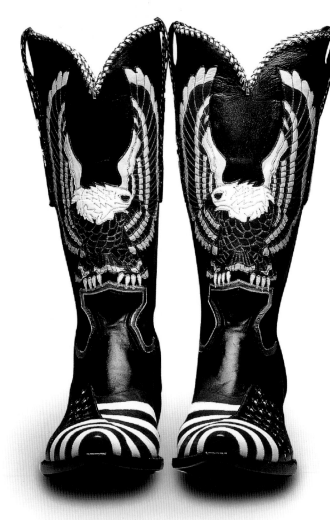

Tres Outlaws; right:
Kimmel Boots;
far right: Country
Cobbler.

wonder: if Betsy Ross or Francis Scott Key popped up today and needed some footwear, would they be shocked and appalled or rush right out and order up some over-the-top, say-it-with-the-USA boots?

Go on and gild yourself a bit or just look at it this way: the American flag and the silhouette of the cowboy boot—perhaps the two most-recognized icons in and exported from the United States—are an obvious match made in boot heaven. If you want to say it loud and proud, say it with flags on your feet.

Clockwise from above: Little's Boots;
J. P.'s Custom Boots; Little's Boots;
opposite: Rocketbuster Boots.

Nudie's, 1960s;
right: Little's Boots.

Boot Garden

In the garden of boots the gathering basket is resplendent and overflowing with variety and color, no matter which way you cut it.

The popularity of flora seems to transcend the gender boundaries and design trends; decade to decade, unfailingly, flowers and vines sway, trail, cling, curl, twirl, and swirl, forever climbing up the boot tops of our imagination, a secret yet shared garden where the seasons never change.

Where do these perennial posies originate from? Can you dig it? Old Mexico, where the sun always shines and

Both pair Sorrell
Custom Boots.

94

the birds and butterflies are free. The Mexican leather craftsmen who wandered into the Texas valley back in the 1930s and '40s brought their talent, traditions, imagination, and profuse color palette. These men were artists, and their designs are still the basis for practically every pair of inlaid, overlaid, and hand-tooled pair of boots made today.

Their beautiful patterns, glow-in-the-dark color combinations in stucco white, lemon yellow, gilded gold, outrageous orange, tranquil topaz, fiery red, burnished blue, mysterious black, and a wall of greens continue to spread joy and gladness, like a garden full of heliotropes. And the only bugs in this leather garden are on the toe.

The two primary techniques employed to create these one- and sometimes three-dimensional mini-murals of nature on leather canvas are inlay and overlay.

With inlay, there is usually, but not always, a basic color on the top and bottom of a pair of boots. Imagine that the color—say black—is solid. Now, if you want to create an inlaid pattern, you would simply cut out a design (shapes) to create holes. When you place a contrasting color behind the black front, those holes, or windows, are now filled with however many colors you wish to show. A simple inlay is one color behind another, but the maestros manage to manipulate leathers in ways that conjure up suspicions of wizardry. Layers and layers of inlay can be applied, one piece on top of another, all thinned (skived) to wafer-like leather sheets for a smoother overall finish.

Overlay on its own, simple and pure, is an application of either the same color of leather, as in black over black, or usually a contrasting color, glued and/or sewn in place. Keep in mind that under that simple overlay, some little or elaborate detail, when applied under overlay, then becomes—you guessed it!—inlay. Confused yet? Well, not to worry. When you design your dream boots, just point to the pictures; the bootmaker can do the rest.

Clockwise from right top: Little's Boots; M. L. Leddy Boots; Little's Boots.

Left, top: M. L. Leddy Boots; left, bottom: Little's Boots; center: M. L. Leddy Boots; far right, top: Little's Boots; far right, bottom: Liberty Boot Company.

Left and above: Liberty Boot Company.

Both pairs: M. L. Leddy
Boot Company.

Left: Liberty Boot Company;
above: Ammons Boots.

Above: Kimmel Boots; right: Little's Boots.

Above: Hyer Boots, 1950s;
right: Zeferino Rios 1960s;
opposite: Trujillo, 1950s.

Vintage 1940–50.

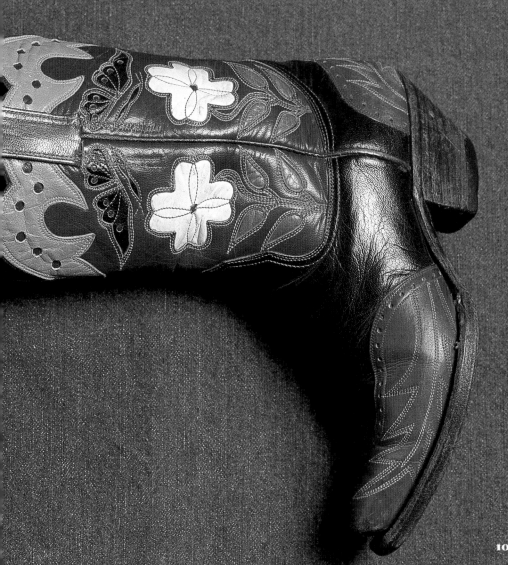

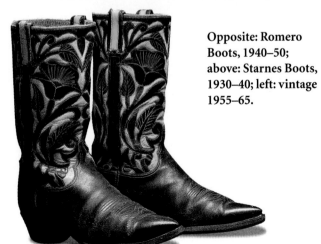

**Opposite: Romero
Boots, 1940–50;
above: Starnes Boots,
1930–40; left: vintage
1955–65.**

Above: vintage 1930–40;
right: vintage 1940–50;
opposite, clockwise from upper left:
Charlie Dunn, 1970s; Hyer Boots 1950s;
Sorrell Custom Boots; Little's Boots.

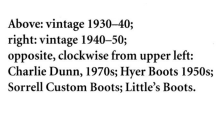

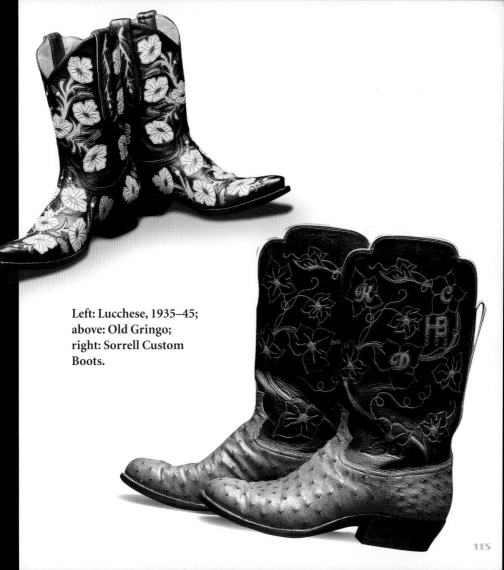

Left: Lucchese, 1935–45;
above: Old Gringo;
right: Sorrell Custom
Boots.

Sorrell Custom Boots; opposite, clockwise from upper left: Charlie Dunn, 1970s; Sorrell Custom Boots; Stephanie Ferguson Custom Boots; Sorrell Custom Boots.

Liberty Boot Company; opposite: Little's Boots.

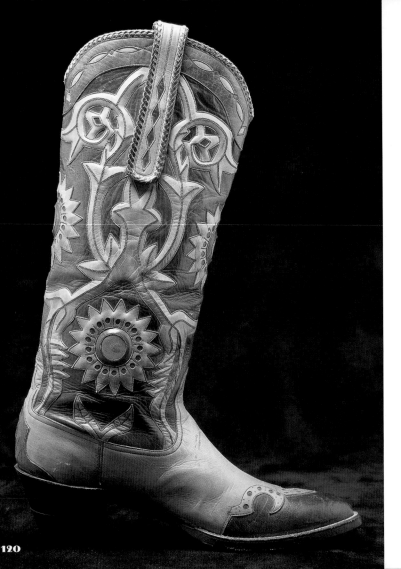

Left: Rios copy
by Larry Mahan,
1970s; right:
vintage 1970–80.

Left: Kimmel Boots;
above: Rocketbuster Boots;
right: vintage 1960s.

Left: Rocketbuster Boots;
right: Little's Boots.

125

Left: vintage 1940s; above: Wild Bill's Boots.

Skulls, Bones,

This pair and opposite: Liberty Boot Company.

Cactus & Critters

People have long been fascinated with imagery of the desert. It is both austere and compelling at the same time. Flowering cacti, desiccated bones, plus any critter that inhabits, scavenges, crawls, slithers, hops, lopes, or runs across the western landscape are ever-popular and recurring themes on the cowboy boot.

For someone who is not personally a desert rat, other fanciful imagery rings with sentiments of the Lone Ranger, "come and get me—I ain't afraid to die," "solitary soul," "the outlaw," and "Lonesome Town"—all creeds for those who see themselves as a little or a lot of rough and tough, perhaps even a survivor of sorts. Whether on the

Little's Boot Company.

Liberty Boot Company.

high seas, prairie, highway, or desert, a certain fraternity has always existed between pirates, outlaws, bikers, and cowboys. These rebels, roustabouts, rounders, and raconteurs have all worn boots.

In the cowboy boot boneyard, no desert dance is complete without the snake, lizard, coyote howlin' at the moon, or "Day of the Dead" skeleton strumming and singing their way through the ether. And the camel? Wrong hemisphere but still qualifies as a desert icon.

As for cowboy pirate boots, I know of just one pair of vintage cowboy boots that had skulls and crossbones—emblazoned in black and white. Those were made

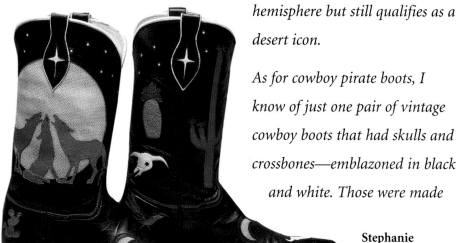

Stephanie Ferguson Custom Boots.

back in 1959 for Mr. Elmer Patton
by Waymon "Tex" Robin, father of
maverick bootmaker Tex Robin.

Little's Boots.

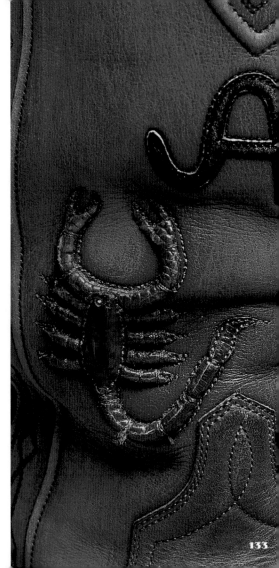

Sorrell Custom Boots.

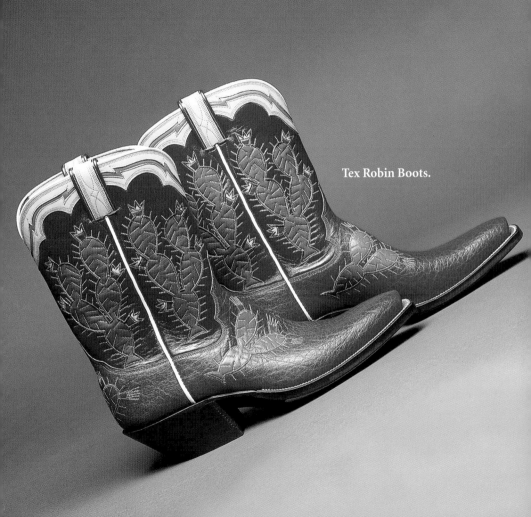

Tex Robin Boots.

Left: Little's Boots; above: Wheeler Boot Company.

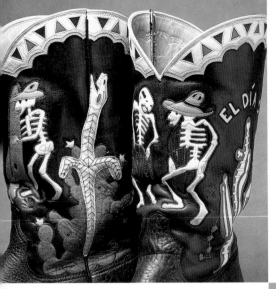

Clockwise from top left:
Wheeler Boot Company;
Little's Boots; Nocona Boot Company
1950s.

Below: M. L. Leddy Boots; right: James Leddy Boot Company.

Tres Outlaws.

Toolin' Around

Hand-tooled cowboy boots are a rare and beautiful thing. For collectors, a pair of these pups is equivalent to the Holy Grail in boot land. The practiced artistry required to complete these "flats" in saddle leather, prepared for construction by a bootmaker or saddle maker, requires decades of dedication and the ability to always sweat the small stuff. There are very few bootmakers who actually tool their own leather. Back in the 1950s and '60s, some saddle makers referred to this work as "playin' around," "piddle work," "something to do while watching TV." Next to a finished saddle this might seem like small taters to some, but these hand-chiseled beauties are consummate works of true art.

Tres Outlaws.

The Mexican

The "dos outlaws" from Tres Outlaws, owners Scott Emmerich and Jerry Black, continue to confound and astound boot enthusiasts. As one of the "seven wonders of the boot-making world," it's no surprise that "The Mexican" won Best Artisan Award in Jewelry and Fashion at the Western Design Conference in 2003. There are dozens of carved and painted beauties, but this pair stands unrivaled, the most paramount eye-dazzler to come down the pike in the realm of the tooled and jeweled. Designed as "a tribute to our neighbors south of the border," Black and carver extraordinaire Ricardo Hernandez conceived and planned the project. This pair of boots is a masterpiece that reflects the rich, evolving culture of Mexico through her struggles and wars, a torch for survival and perseverance. The laborious layout took more than 100 hours, the detail-intensive tooling more than 300 hours, and the brilliant brushwork in a plethoric palette in excess of 200. Bezeled and buried in and among it all are twenty-two rare Mexican coins from both gold and silver strikes. But the pièce de resistance is the 400 lemon-wood pegs used to finish and finesse the soles with visions of Aztec temple art and mysterious inscriptions.

Rocketbuster Boots.

Variations on these chiseled and chamfered, cut and divided, hand-hewed, indented and sliced, and sometimes painted conversation pieces are limitless. Many pairs are ornamented with silver conchos, coins, buckle sets, or jewelry. Initials and brands, even pastimes and hobbies can be depicted with the overall effect being that of a mural. Rocketbuster Boots recently completed matching pairs of hand-tooled and -painted "family portrait" boots—complete with the pets—for movie director Steven Spielberg and his actress wife, Kate Capshaw. George Lucas (Star Wars) was inspired by theirs to order his own pair of "my life in leather." Many a tooled boot is laced or buck-stitched to create a decorative border or margin achieved through single, double, triple, or even candy-striped plait design.

In the early 1990s, there was only a smattering of carved and painted vintage or contemporary boots to be found. It was the (late and lamented) Bob Dellis masterworks displayed in Art of the Boot *(1992) that really got the bootmakers, toolers, and customers all worked up. Suddenly, everybody wanted a pair of personalized, hand-tooled cowboy boots. Bob's touch* was light but heavily detailed; he was fond of floral wraparound one-piece tops with depictions of western scenes, towns, and desertscapes. Up until this time, most themes had been floral and basket weave, with perhaps a brand or a set of initials. Bob revived the skills of two-tone, triple, and even quadruple staining in order to secure depth perception and accentuate the incisions and stippled backgrounds. Lately it seems that every tooler of "smalls" and every saddle maker is tooling boot tops. But the guys that are putting out the bulk of the hand-tooled booty are leather maestros Jim Resley, Shirley Robinson, Ray Pohja, Howard Knight, John Simon, Lefty, and Ricardo Hernandez and his phenomenal crew at Tres Outlaws.

What makes these artisan boots all so irresistible is their tactile element. Their texture and painted-leather appeal is positively infectious. As with tattoos, anything goes—kooky and kitschy, grand and glorious, or subtle and simple. Finesse a dream, memory, or fantasy in leather and Technicolor tints. There is no time like the present to present yourself with a present of cool hand-tooled cowboy boots.

Rocketbuster
Boots.

"The Forty Roses of Our Lady of Guadalupe"

This immaculate conception could only be another masterwork by cowboy boot connoisseurs Tres Outlaws. This particular "lady" pair was an inspired Christmas gift idea by bootologist Jim Arndt for his sweetest of hearts, Nathalie Kent, a fine boot designer herself. The ecclesiastical endeavor was the burgeoning brainchild of Outlaw Scott Emmerich. A personal inspiration for the creation and execution of the Lady boots sprang from a childhood fascination with the religious iconography he could not shake from his artistic consciousness. For him, "the roses seemed to float and were free at the base of Our Lady's figure." A staggering 400 hours went into the creation of these highest on high heels. This pair is definitely one of "the seven wonders of the boot-making world."

Opposite: Little's Boots; this page: Liberty Boot Company.

**Above: Tres Outlaws;
right: Little's Boots.**

Little's Boots; right: Kimmel Boots.

Sorrell Custom Boots.

Lefty's Leathercraft.

Little's Boots.

Kimmel Boots.

159

Above: Rocketbuster Boots; opposite, clockwise from top left: Little's Boots; Rocketbuster Boots; Kimmel Boots; Liberty Boot Company.

J. P.'s Custom Boots.

Liberty Boot Company.

Vintage 1940s.

Ty Skiver Boots.

163

Left: Tres Outlaws.

Above: Liberty Boot Company;
left: Little's Boots.

**Right: Little's Boots;
below: vintage 1940s.**

Texas Traditions.

Above and right: Little's Boots.

Saddle Up

Saddle up and be beguiled by this prairie-sized passel of perforated and punched, high-falutin' boodle of cowboy "theme" boots. Before 1920, sumptuous saddles, cowboys and vaqueros on frisky buckin' broncs, bull portraits, horseshoes, and longhorns simply were not seen on boots. It was not until after the dime novels, latter-day Wild West shows, and the romanticization of the cow punchers who blazed the cattle trails north to the Kansas railheads, that the symbology of the West began to proliferate.

These icons were popular not just for boots, but in the marketing of products of every description: soaps, sardines, or saddles—it made no difference; anything stamped with cowboy lithography sold. Along with the horses and cattle on boots came the moon and stars. Even today it's

the cowboy's wide-open sky that we all dream of and envy. By the 1940s, boots for men, women, and children were bubbling up with all the basic elements in leitmotif that western dreams are made of.

Okay, so you missed the cattle drives and you've never roped a steer. Your chance to get near to it all is in a pair of flamboyantly designed boot creations, fashion's answer for the suburban dude or dudette that pounds more mall dust than prairie dust.

Left and right: Little's Boots.

Left: Little's Boots; above: children's boots, vintage 1935–45.

Both pair, vintage 1950s–60s.

Don Quixote Boot Company 1950–60.

Vintage 1950–60.

Left: Paul Bond Boot Company;
below: Hyer Boots, 1940–50.

Left: child's vintage 1930–40; above: Liberty Boot Company.

Below: Zeferino Rios, 1950–60;
right: Justin Boots, 1954;
opposite: Little's Boots.

Left: Lucchese, 1950s; this page: vintage 1940s.

Little's Boots;
right: vintage 1940–50.

Above: vintage 1955–65;
right: Rios Boots 1950s;
opposite: Tres Outlaws.

Left: Kimmel Boots; above: vintage 1940s.

Above left: Rocketbuster Boots; right: child's Acme, 1950s.

Clockwise from top left: Little's Boots, 1950–60; Paul Bond Boot Company; vintage 1950s; Little's Boots, 1950–60.

Vintage
1950s.

Vintage 1935–45.

Left: vintage 1920–30;
below: Rocketbuster Boots;
right: Ty Skiver Boots.

Tres Outlaws; opposite:
Rocketbuster Boots.

ings that Fly

The custom bootmaker's felicitous abilities are no better showcased than in these flights of fancy. In fact, there's no better place for fledgling boot collectors to start than right here, smack dab in the core of the sane and the insane, the witty, the whimsical, the wacky—all wrapped up in and around things that fly.

Butterflies, eagles, hummingbirds, hawks, the mythic thunderbird, owls, red birds, blue birds, vultures, pink flamingoes, and even UFOs: as with almost all boot designs, an innocent androgyny seems to prevail.

Don't get your feathers all ruffled, but historically, men have owned more

Above: Deanna McGuffin; left: Tres Outlaws

boots with butterflies and flowers, delicately cut out in collisions of madcap, carnival, and circusy colors than women. Bird and butterfly imagery have decorously appeared on boots since the 1920s. Wings just look great, and they fit and fill the space of a boot top perfectly. They are visually a vainglorious way to set oneself apart from the melding masses. When it comes to cowboy boots, guys are given the right to get a little wild under the pants leg, and even "over" for the braver of heart. What's good for the goose seems to be good for the gander.

Wheeler Boot Company.

Opposite: Tex Robin Boots;
above: vintage 1950s;
left: Frank's Boot Shop,
1940–50.

Above and opposite: all vintage 1950–60.

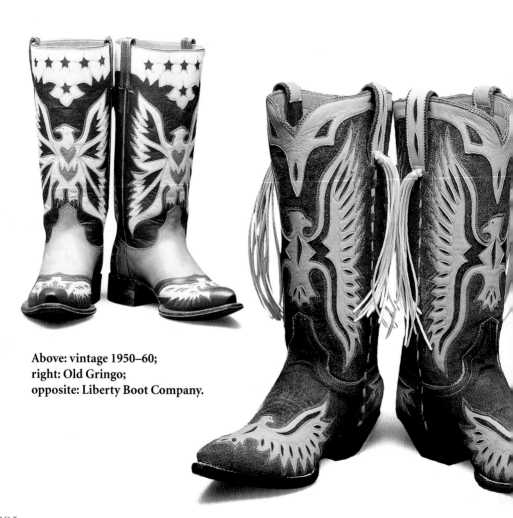

Above: vintage 1950–60;
right: Old Gringo;
opposite: Liberty Boot Company.

Tres Outlaws;
opposite, clockwise from
top left: Rudy Rios, 1980s;
vintage 1940s; vintage
1930–40; Liberty Boot
Company.

Left: Old Gringo; above: vintage 1930–40.

Left: Economy Boot Shop, 1940-50;
above: vintage 1940–50.

Pascal Boots.

Above: vintage 1945–55;
left: Romero Boots 1940–50;
right: Rios Boots, 1950s.

Left: Romero, 1940–50;
right: vintage 1950–60.

All vintage
1930–40.

Left: Rios Boots, 1950s;
right: Tres Caballos, 1955–65;
below: vintage 1940s.

Above: vintage 1940–50;
right: vintage 1950s;
opposite: vintage 1940–50.

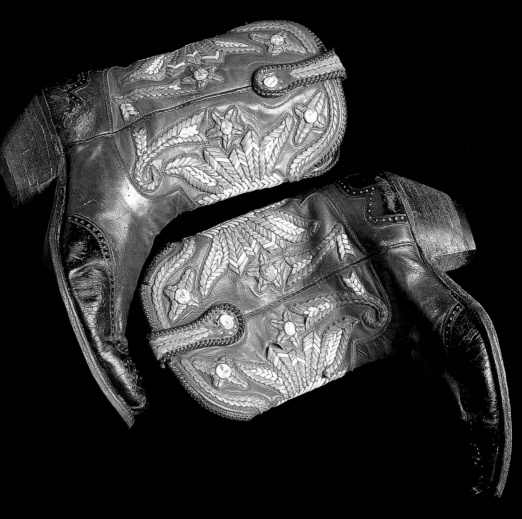

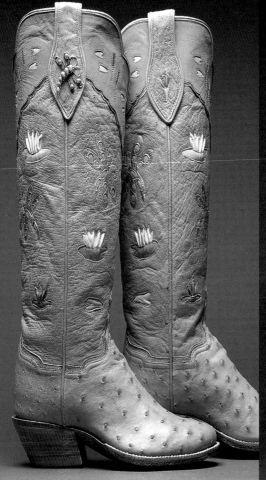

Stephanie Ferguson Custom Boots.

Little's Boots.

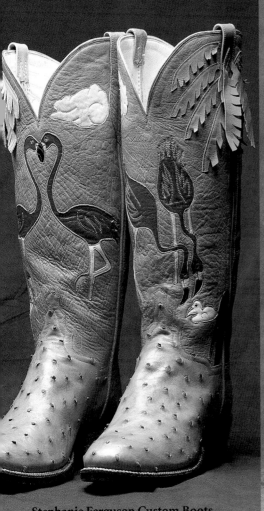

Stephanie Ferguson Custom Boots.

Texas Traditions.

Rios Boots,
1955–65.

Rocketbuster Boots.

Vintage 1950s;
opposite: Nocona Boots, Texas
State Fair display, 1950s.

Tantalizing Toes

Like buildings, boots have traditional proportions and pleasing shapes, but when it comes to the toes, anything goes! Toes are the imperial elixir of the boot. They tell folks a little about who you are, where you have been, and where you're going; they provide a clue but not the whole answer. Cowboy boots can sometimes be a mellifluous creation, or the toes can belie some artistic masterwork that lies in wait above the ankle line. Some toes simply point, pout, or shout; others are boisterous, braggy, and boastful.

One bootmaker recounted that he dreads the moment while taking a custom order when the client has to decide on a toe. Tension mounts; people get all flustered and fussy, he explained.

All Tres Outlaws.

Once he spouted out, "Well, do you want some sort of smarty shape or perhaps an amphibious landing shape—would that work for you?"

Boots have reflected changes in the history of the world and the toes always got there first, so to speak. Over the past century or so, toes have ranged from traditional, time-tested classics to trippy and tasty. For example, pre-1920 cowboy boots had wide square and narrow rounded shapes; in the 1930s and '40s they begin to snub off, and the "boxed" toe got its fashionable foothold. For nearly thirty years, men, women, and children wore blunted toes in the

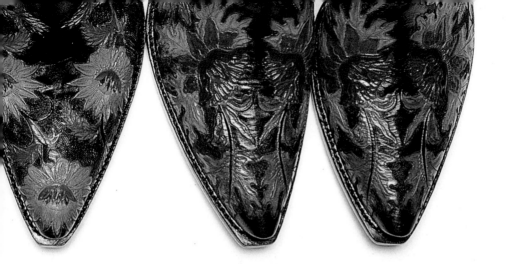

familiar measurements of quarter-inch box, five-eighths-inch box, and one-inch box; some even wore duck-billed toes up to two inches across. One classy profile from the 1940s and '50s is the high heel with an inward slope, an angle that opposes the same angle on the little box toe: it's called "undershot" on the toe and "underslung" on the heel.

By the late 1950s, everything was coming up streamlined and modernized, just like Cadillac fins. The old boxed toe had to go, and in a trice, everyone was strutting home in the "needle-nose" toe—all the same shape, give or

Tres Outlaws.

Liberty Boot Company.

take a fraction of an inch. And, yes, "real cowboys" did wear pointed toes, from the late '50s right up to about 1970. Museum archives document it.

The mellower 1970s brought forth the more rounded toes, the "J-toe," "H-toe," the "half-round," the " full-round," "the paddle-foot," and the modified and revised "French toe," which bowed in the front and dipped a little on its sides. Once the bootmakers and the factories realized how much easier it was to fashion and last a toe that was not narrow and pointed, they began to throw away their old foot forms. So, by 1980, when the suburban Urban Cowboy craze took off, toes got rounder and rounder. Bootmakers were having to stitch, sole, seam, and finish boots at an unprecedented and frenetic pace. Time was money, and the rounder the toe, the more time was saved. Enter "the roper," which in the 1950s was stuck in the back of the catalogs as the cheapest, plainest work boot; again, with the easiest toe to form, this little pup was called "the Wellington."

The toe is a great placed to go when you want to create fun, colorful overlay and inlay designs. The technique is called "foxing the toe."

Vintage 1950s.

Nudie's, 1960s.

Above: Little's Boots; below, left: vintage 1955–65; below, right: Bo Riddle Boots.

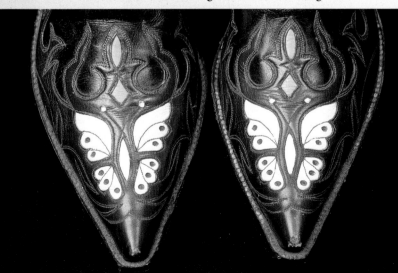

Above and right: Tres Outlaws.

Left: Rocketbuster Boots; above: vintage 1950s; right: Liberty Boot Company.

The heel is either the height of fashion or the form of function. The ideal heel for most men and women achieves a little altitude and attitude while maintaining a cushion and a comfort zone.

Let's talk cowboy heel history for a minute. Contrary to popular belief, many a working cowboy took great pride in his appearance, and a fair amount of thought went into his attire and accoutrements, especially if he would be in a town on Saturday night with the ladies. Museums and private collections are full of flashy western wear—beaded, hand-carved, embroidered, buckled and belted, plaited and studded. Many a cowpoke got elevated, got more cattle, and probably got more girls in his high-heeled boots.

Left: vintage 1930–40; right: Tres Outlaws.

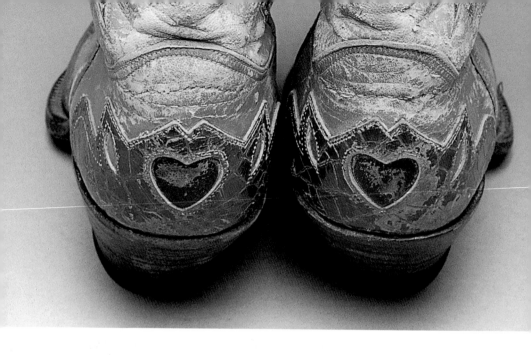

The fact is, heel appeal is all part of the mutual admiration society between the sexes. A heel, whether your thing is a low flat walker, a waisted wonder, a square squat, a flirtatious flair, a come-hither Cuban, a spiraling spike, a platformed plateau, or an ungrounded, undershot sweetie with barely enough rubber pad to cover a quarter, a good set of heels can make the

Vintage 1940–50.

man or accentuate the feminine. Heels make the wearer appear more—or less—powerful; they can elate and elevate.

Some women are sex-conscious about their heels. In fact, the architecture of a heel is compared to various parts of the female anatomy (see page 315): after all, heels are curvaceous, graceful, easy on the eyes—but for fashion slaves, hard on the feet. High heels can be for dancing or daring; their come-hither tap, tap, tap is an enticing invitation.

Without a doubt, men are simply jealous of the fanciful and extensive choices women are offered in the world of footwear. Cowboy boots give guys a chance to wear bright colors and high heels. Regardless of the boost or bounce, whether you're ratcheted up or those leather elevators really don't go all the way to the top, here's the deal: the boot stops here and the choice is yours.

Joe Bowman and Sam DeGeorge, 1950s; opposite, top: vintage 1930–40; bottom: Rocketbuster Boots.

Above: Rudy Rios; below:
Liberty Boot Company.

246

Clockwise from top left: vintage Tom Mix, 1920s; Nocona, 1930s; Michael Anthony; Paul Bond Boot Company.

Tres Outlaws; opposite: Nudie's, 1955–65.

James Leddy Boot
Company.

Heart & Sole

Cowboy boots seem to have a direct line to our hearts. They touch our souls and serve as canvas for a mood, a moment, or a whim. They may express our feelings about an experience, event, or epiphany of some sort. Ordering custom boots becomes a gratifying experience of self-expression.

While purchasing a pair "off the rack" may not be as personal, it can still be exciting and satisfying. Women are renowned for shoe shopping to cure what ails them, but when it comes to boots, there is no division of the sexes. A brand-spanking-new pair of boots is exactly what the Doctor of Bootology recommends. More than a few collectors firmly believe that a different

pair on the feet every day will keep the doctor away (Dr. Scholl maybe . . .).
At any rate, everyone needs at least one pair that rocks their world; invokes
or erupts some locked-up emotion or desire; records, in the language of

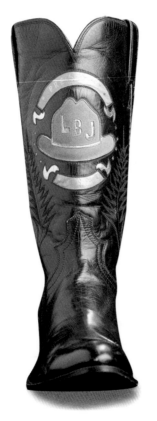

leather, who you are, where you've been, and where you're going.

Say it with a pair of wedding boots, birthday boots, logo boots, a portrait of the kids, a ranch brand, or a favorite flower. Make a religious stand; stand by your state with a flag. Tickle the tools of your bootmaker by requesting the tools of your trade. Create mysterious petroglyphs, a cryptic message, a love letter, or a holiday diary of hand-tooled symbols.

Lucchese, 1960s.

Rocketbuster Boots.

Whether black and white, a glorious spectrum of color, or gilded with shimmer and shine, cowboy boots are the tattoos of our souls on soles. Designing your own is a coalescent venture, a partnership with your bootmaker, where some elements are borrowed but where there is always room for something new.

Boots have an ageless appeal. Cowboy charisma and couture, something citizen Joe and citizen Jane share in common with a slue of celebrities who have sported stylish boots—
Oprah Winfrey,

Left, top: Paul Bond Boot Company; bottom: Liberty Boot Company; right: M. L. Leddy Boots.

Arnold Schwarzenegger, Bruce Willis, Sharon Stone, Billy Bob Thornton, Jennifer Tilly, Tommy Lee Jones, Mel Gibson, Hillary Duff, Nicole Kidman, Eric Clapton, Ralph Lauren and fellow fashion designers Yoshi Yamamoto and Catherine Malandrino, as well as an endless who's who of fleet-footed politicians and pop and country music stars.

Boot bliss knows no economic downturn. Priorities in place, the price is always relative: affordable boots or drop-dead glamour at a cost—take your pick. The fervor and vivacity that a pair of cowboy boots can instill will forever be linked with attitude and high fashion. Boots come sex-packed and full of outlaw euphoria. Whether you settle in a pair of complex killers, arresting thrillers, stunners that scream out loud, eye-poppin', traffic stoppin', mind boggling, or drop-your-jaw-and-go-apoplectic boots, they can serve you walking or set you up for gawking. Even if you simply saunter in a pair of simmering exotics or slither yourself down into a pair of pearlized leather sweeties, if the boot fits your mind, body, and soul— wear it!

Rocketbuster Boots.

Today it's a passionate sort of pleasure to monitor the foot fashions forged by skilled artisans: electric embroideries, brilliant baroque beadwork, stitched stingers, inlays and overlays that rival and mimic the old-world artist's champlevé and cloisonné, jewels, and liquid gold and silver formed into conchos and coins. Leather filigrees of every description, hand-painted and hand-tooled, have closed in on the classics and broken all the rules. We now find ourselves immersed in a timeless wonderland of boots.

We aren't simply in the "new renaissance" but have now entered the "double platinum" age of the cowboy boot.

From top to bottom and tip to toe, these boots will tug at your heart and trip their way into your soul. Behold the cowboy boot: long live their makers.

Opposite: James Leddy Boot Company; left: Sorrell Custom Boots.

Left: Texas Traditions; below: Tres Outlaws; right: vintage 1950s.

Above: Kimmel Boots; opposite: Liberty Boot Company.

Clockwise from top left:
Melody's Custom Boots;
Rocketbuster Boots; vintage
1940–50.

Vintage 1940s.

Tlo Lowery.

Clockwise from bottom:
Liberty Boot Company;
Old Gringo; J. B. Hill
Boot Company.

Vintage 1950–60; right: Deanna
McGuffin; far right: L. W. McGuffin.

Left: Liberty Boot Company; right: William Shanor and Julie Bonney; opposite, left: vintage 1950s; right: vintage 1940–50.

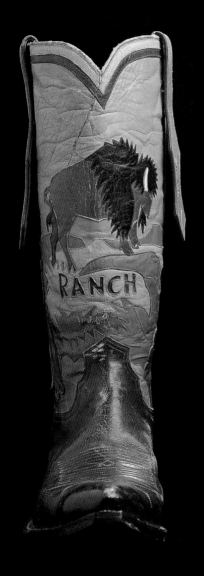
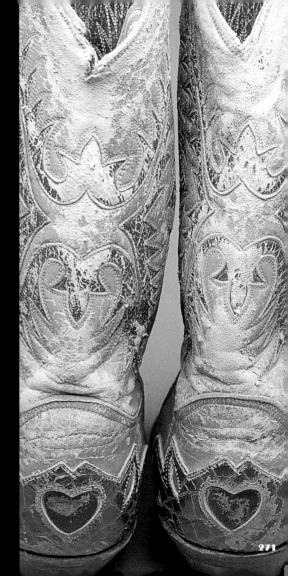

Wheeler Boot Company;
right: Paul Bond Boot Company;
far right: M. L. Leddy Boots.

Opposite: Lucchese, 1950s.
Above: M. L. Leddy Boots;
left: Paul Bond Boot Company.

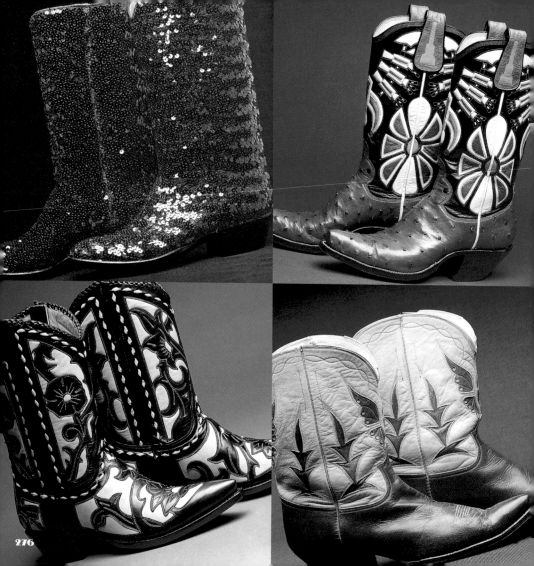

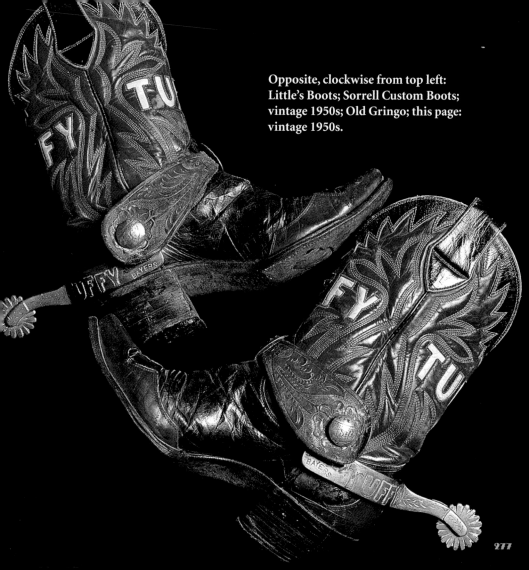

Opposite, clockwise from top left:
Little's Boots; Sorrell Custom Boots;
vintage 1950s; Old Gringo; this page:
vintage 1950s.

Opposite: Nocona Boots, 1940s; left: Sorrell Custom Boots; below left: Paul Bond Boot Company; below right: M. L. Leddy Boots.

Liberty Boot Company.

Vintage 1940s.

Above: vintage pre-1930;
right: Tres Outlaws;
opposite, left: vintage 1955–60;
opposite, right: Olsen-Stelzer, 1940s.

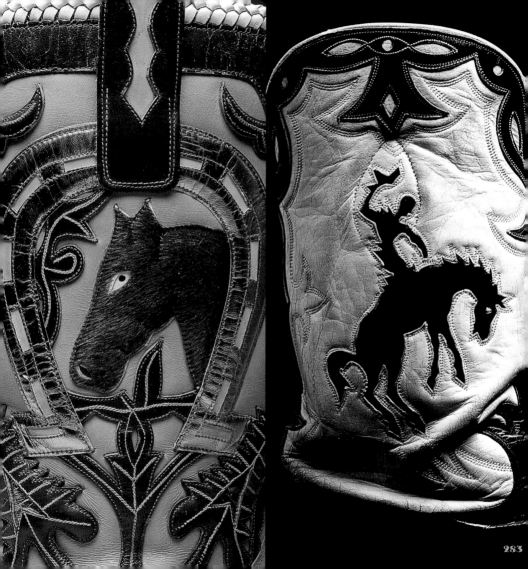

Nudie's, 1960s.

Texas Traditions.

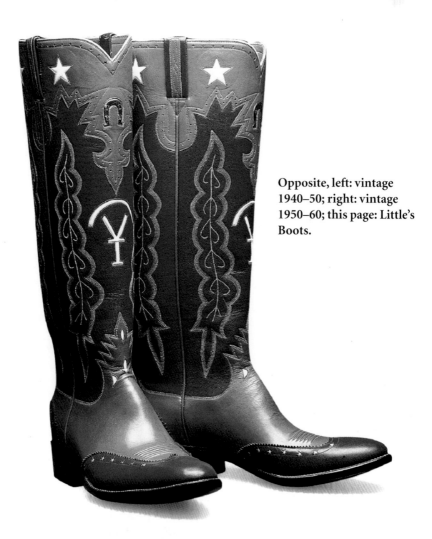

Opposite, left: vintage 1940–50; right: vintage 1950–60; this page: Little's Boots.

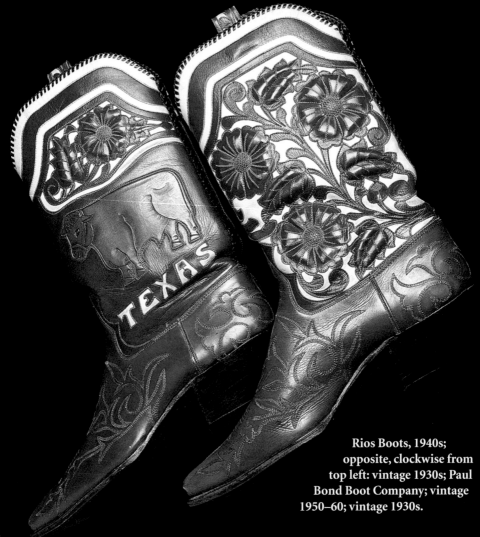

Rios Boots, 1940s; opposite, clockwise from top left: vintage 1930s; Paul Bond Boot Company; vintage 1950–60; vintage 1930s.

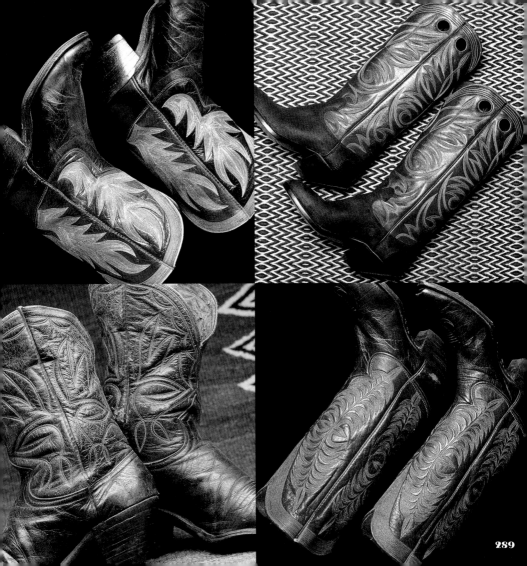

Left and below: Little's Boots;
center: vintage 1960–70;
opposite: vintage 1950s.

**Stephanie Ferguson Custom Boots; opposite:
Rocketbuster and Rocket "Baby" Buster.**

Left: Rocketbuster Boots; above:
vintage 1950–60; opposite:
vintage pair, 1950s.

Tex Robin Boots.

Kimmel Boots;
opposite: Nocona Boots,
1940–50.

Opposite: Little's Boots;
above: Rocketbuster Boots.

Opposite: Paul Bond Boot Company;
this page, top row: Liberty Boot
Company; bottom: Kimmel Boots.

Left: vintage 1950–60;
this page: Liberty Boot
Company.

Opposite: James Leddy
Boot Company; this page:
Tres Outlaws.

Boot Camp

I have worn cowboy boots all my life. My first pair at age three were custom red and green inlays, a 1957 Christmas gift from Mom and Pop. As I began to sprout like all preteens do, I was plopped into store-bought, stock-size, rough-out, indestructible clodhoppers (bear in mind, this was 1965, so they had a pointed toe). Growing children are usually encouraged to wear boots one size too large, to "grow into." At age nineteen, I designed my first adult pair of custom boots. They felt too tight, so the maker stretched them and then they were fine. In retrospect, they were probably a perfect fit to begin with, but being used to a sloppy-fitting boot, I reacted too quickly. Now, after more than 250 pairs of custom boots, I guarantee that once a bootmaker has your last (a wooden or fiberglass foot mold) honed to perfection, you will be able to wear your boots eighteen hours a day and never even know they're on your feet unless you look down.

The perfect fit is very subjective, of course. A bootmaker will gaze down at your feet, swimming or bulging in your existing boots, and give an opinion about what is good and bad about your current state of foot affairs. But in the end, you are the one who wears the boot, and you alone must decide what is comfortable for you. Listen to the maker, but be firm—you are buying art, but it is supposed to be wearable and painless. It's always better to get your first pair a hair too loose than a hair too tight.

The human foot is comprised of twenty-eight bones encased by numerous muscles, nerve endings, and blood vessels. Yet feet have an acute and peculiar ability to absorb stress and strain. A person's weight, the way one walks, one's profession, what one walks in, and good old genetics all have a profound impact on the physical condition of one's feet. Even with all their forgiveness and strength, how many times have you heard people say "My dogs are barkin'"? Our poor old feet hold us up all our lives; they work hard. It's about time they got some respect, attention, and fanciful footwear.

Cowboy boots feel and fit differently from shoes: most shoes have little or no arch support, but cowboy boots do. Therefore, some breaking-in time may be required—a few weeks tops! The old rule of thumb is still a good one: as you pull on the boot, there should be a little whoosh and a pop as you enter the foot area. Once inside, there should be a little movement in the heel, but you shouldn't be slippin' and slidin' all over the place. The instep is the part of your foot between your heel and the top of the foot. This area is what determines how well you stay in your "seat," not the length of the boot so much. The toe shape should have no impact whatsoever on the way a boot fits. Even pointed "cockroach killer" toes are a decorative extension to make the foot appear sexier or slimmer. Whether it's a paddle foot, a half-round, or a needle nose, the toe should not affect the fit.

However, even a sixteenth of an inch difference in a measurement or the variation of thickness in hides can be felt by an experienced boot wearer. It's not a big deal, but you can feel it nevertheless. A simple procedure to remedy this is to wear a thicker or thinner sock, and presto!—all your boots feel exactly the same. Some folks like putting in a gel or cushioned insert if they prefer wearing thin socks yet want to feel really snugged up.

If, after a week or so of daily wear, anything about your boots is bothering you, perhaps an adjustment is in order. Most custom makers will tell you that 10 to 15 percent of their boots are returned because the customer needs minor, or sometimes major, adjustments. There are almost always first-time buyers who are accustomed to wearing loafers or sneakers or tromping around in bare feet and simply do not understand how a boot should fit. All boots can be stretched a little bit in most areas. Over-the-counter sprays and ointments are seldom satisfactory. The best policy is to return the boots to the maker for these fine tunings. Never take them to a local shoe or boot repairer who has no personal investment in those boots, and who may not have the standard equipment for those procedures.

If you already know how boots are supposed to fit, they should be comfortable from the moment you slip them on, and you should expect additional enjoyment in the wearing as they break in more and more, just like your favorite pair of jeans. Above all, there should never be any pain involved, not even on day one.

When shopping for a bootmaker, it's preferable to visit them in person. If at all possible, plan a tour of the boot shops while on vacation or a business trip. This way you have the opportunity to meet the makers in person, see and handle their work, and determine if this is the bootmaker custom made for you. Getting measured in person, especially the first time, is always better.

If you don't have the luxury of a personal visit, choose a maker or two whose designs you find appealing. Call, write, E-mail, or fax, inquiring if they do mail orders and whether they have a measurement chart and instructions they can send you. Some shops will only take orders in person; others will only do standard stock sizes by mail. With a custom fit, the maker will take about eight measurements. Custom-made cowboy boots are not a science; they are a wearable art form. Taking a proper measurement takes from 15 to 45 minutes, depending on the maker. They all have a system. In my experience, one is no better than another. Bottom line: the boot has to fit, be comfy, and painless from the first try-on.

If you are ordering by mail, you will be asked what size boot you normally wear, and possibly to provide a tracing of your feet for a double-check. Some makers will supply you with a packet of information and guide you through the entire process. I also have known a few first-timers who actually sent an old pair of boots that they liked (or possibly didn't like) so they could be analyzed. From a well-worn pair of boots, a maker can determine how you walk and the way you shift your weight—front to back or side to side. They can see if you are tough on your footwear or light on your feet.

Designing the finished boot. Each boot's outside appearance is an ever-changing canvas for your imagination—a sublime form of self-expression. Decide what you want by looking through this awe-inspiring book as well as *Art of the Boot, 100 Years of Western Wear,* and *The Cowboy Boot Book* (all collaborations by Beard and Arndt). Glean your inspirations slowly, but be sensible. It is easy to get wowed. Resist trying to put everything your little ole heart desires on one single pair of boots. A few bootmakers also have their own catalogs that might also help get the boot ball rolling.

Now that you're ready to order, ask for leather samples to look at, colors of thread, perhaps a few photocopies of stitch patterns, toe bugs, toe shapes, and heel shapes with their seemingly endless widths, heights, and angles. A good bootmaker will communicate with you on every detail to insure complete satisfaction. Although every artist has his or her temperament, pride, and vision, you should also seek design advice from the bootmaker: after all, he has seen it all and done it all, and usually knows what works and what doesn't.

Don't be affronted if you are asked to sign the order; this is insurance for both of you and will prevent later disputes over minute details. An initial deposit of half is usually standard, with the balance due upon final fitting.

How to care for your boots and lengthen their life. A store-bought boot will last maybe a year under heavy wear, but a custom boot with superior materials inside and out will last four to five times longer. Here are some tips for care: remember, cows spend their lives outside, as do most critters from whose hides boots are made. Even a tanned hide is durable, semi-weather resistant, yet retains "live" properties. My personal regime is to always wipe the dust and grime off my boots with a slightly warm, damp cotton cloth or old sock. I tend to polish and buff about every third time I wear a pair of boots. The ideal, of course, is that you clean them after every wearing with a little saddle soap and tepid water, provided that you hand-dry the boots with a soft cloth afterwards. Never set a pair of wet boots by a heat source or an open fire. After the boots are thoroughly dry, they can be wiped down with a neutral or compatible-color conditioning cream. Avoid sticky, gooey, waterproofing products; they will do no service to the leather. If you nick the leather, you can touch it up with a cotton swab and a matching colored cream, then buff and polish. Most exotic hides can be treated with a neutral leather conditioner, BUT always ask your bootmaker for his or her own personal product preference and care procedures. Personal responsibility to your boots and your bootmaker's expertise will make it possible to get the maximum life expectancy out of your boots. Custom boots are expensive, so take care of them—y'all hear? Having said all that, everyone should have one sacrificial pair of custom boots—the pair you never treat or condition; the pair you want to look like you've been working cattle for days and put yourself up wet in; that lovely pair that sits slumped by the door, rough and ready and waiting.

I have had some of my boots re-soled six or seven times before the foot leather finally gave out. Another secret is that the maker can simply re-foot the boots: the tops will probably last a lifetime, unless you work in manure or chemicals or stretch barbed-wire fence on a daily basis. It's a simple procedure to put a new foot on the old top. You can even change the color, hide, or details as long as the tongue pattern remains the same and the size is not altered much. Some bootmakers simply refuse to do this, none of them like to—but it can be done for about half the price of a new pair.

The toe can't be changed unless a boot is re-footed, but a heel can be altered at any time. While there is a certain amount of built-in heel-height variance based on the last that the bootmaker used, the angle of the back can be sheared off to any desired slope.

Once you fall head over heels for your first pair, you'll be wanting to order a second. One of the best pieces of advice I've ever received came from my fellow bootist Evan Voyles, who suggested that if I loved everything about a particular pair of boots, I should simply have them copied. For years I insisted on mucking up the design, adding and deleting, basically trying to get too much on one pair of boots. Caution: if you try to play Picasso when designing your own boots, the result could either be a masterpiece or a mess! Either way, if they are what you ordered and they fit, you own 'em!

In this day and age, anything custom made is a precious luxury, and cowboy boots are certainly no exception. Today's bootmaker is a reflection of a time in this country when everyone had a profession, a trade that set them apart as an expert at something—a time when hard work, intuition, talent, and basic blood, sweat, and tears resulted in quality goods and decorative yet functional works of art. Ordering a pair of custom boots should be an exciting experience, a personal artistic odyssey, an event. So get out your boot books, colored pens, or computer graphics and go berserk! Long live the cowboy boot and its makers!

Boot Anatomy

Pull strap

Piping (beading)

Scallop

Collar

Inlay

Back quarter

Counter

Heel base

Heel waist

Heel cap

Outsole

Side seam with piping, or side welt

Top front quarter or boot shaft

Waist

Tongue

Instep

Heel breast

Outsole stitching

Vamp foxing

The Bootmakers

We did our level best to find each and every one of you, but it has been a job. So, if you move, close up shop, merge, or if any of the particulars are incorrect or we simply missed you this go-round, drop me a line and we will try to get your information right on the next printing. You may contact me at Tyler Beard, P.O. Box 1286, Lampasas, Texas 76550. If you make a pair of plucky or flashy boots that cry out to be seen in upcoming cowboy boot books or calendars, contact Jim Arndt for instructions at (612) 332-5050. All makers listed here take custom orders; asterisk indicates stock sizes also available.

★ A ★

Acox Custom Boots
Oswalt Rd
Overbrook, OK 73453
(580) 276-5678

*Alberta Boot Company
614-10th Ave SW
Calgary, AB, Canada
T2R-1M3
(403) 263-4605

Alta Boots
3005 East Center Street
Anderson, CA 96007
(530) 378-2698

Amado Boot Company
734-2nd
Mercedes, TX 78570
(956) 565-9641

*Ammons Boots
1477 Lomaland St, C-9
El Paso, TX 79935
(915) 595-2100

Angelo Boot Shop
37 West Twohig St
San Angelo, TX 76903
(325) 486-9544

*Austin-Hall Boot Company
230 Chelsea St
El Paso, TX 79905
(915) 771-6113

★ B ★

**B & D Custom Boots
& Leather**
HCR 4, Box 1200
Burnet, TX 78611
(512) 756-1772

*Back at the Ranch
209 E Marcy
Santa Fe, NM 87501
(505) 989-8110
*Features the Tyler Beard Boot
Collection*

Backyard Boots
16090 NE Spencer
Fletcher, OK 73541
(580) 281-0079

Beck Cowboy Boots
723 S Georgia
Amarillo, TX 79106
(806) 373-1600

Best Little Boot Shop
2434 Azel Ave
Ft. Worth, TX 76106
(817) 626-8517

Big Star Boots
3020 El Cerrito Plaza,
PMB 273
El Cerrito, CA 94530
(510) 435-5863

*Billy Martin's
8605 W Sunset Blvd
Hollywood, CA 90069
(310) 289-5000

*Billy Martin's
220 E 60th St
New York, NY 10022
(212) 308-7272

Bishop's Handmade Boots
PO Box 14
Tucumcari, NM 88401
(505) 461-1889

Blucher Custom Boots
103 S Maple at Hwy 16
Beggs, OK 74421
(918) 267-5393

Bo Riddle Boots
517 N 21st
Ozark, MO 65721
(417) 582-2668

Boden Custom Boots
117-A CR 353
Merkel, TX 79536
(325) 669-9533

Boehm Boots
16830 Pine Lake Rd
Walton, NE 68461
(402) 782-2179

Boot Hill Custom Footwear
19263 Gilliat Ave
Council Bluff, IA 51503
(712) 322-1789

Boots by Joe
Rt. 1, Box 780
Webbers Falls, OK 74470
(918) 989-5433

Bowman Boots
307 E 10th St
Bridgeport, NE 69336
(308) 262-1228

*Bowman's Wilson's Boots
1014 West Park, #5
Livingston, MT 59047
(406) 222-3842

Brangier Custom Boots
7664 Blueberry Acres Rd
St. Michaels, MD 21663
(410) 745-6249

Brown's Boot & Saddle
Rt. 1, Box 441
Paradise, TX 76073
(940) 433-9960

Brunson Boots
113 S Third
Artesia, NM 88210
(505) 748-3201

*Buffalo Chips
426 Washington St
New York, NY 10013
(212) 965-0300

Burk Boot Shop
206 E Third
Burkburnett, TX 76354
(940) 569-4990

Burton's Boot & Saddlery
120 N Main
Roswell, NM 88201
(505) 622-6424

Buster & Company
8285-68th St SW
Staples, MN 56479
(218) 397-2401

C. T. Boot Shop
(Teaches)
105 S Main
Saint Jo, TX 76265
(940) 995-2901

Capitol Saddlery
1614 Lavaca
Austin, TX 78701
(512) 478-9309

Carlos Boot Shop
10844 Westheimer Rd
Houston, TX 77042
(713) 977-6347

Carmack's Custom Boots
PO Box 149
Glen Rose, TX 76043
(254) 897-2176

Carmargo's of Mercedes
710 Hwy 83
Mercedes, TX 78570
(956) 565-6457

Case Trade Boot
PO Box 157
Eagleville, MO 64442
(660) 867-3121

*Cavazos Boot Factory
302-2nd St
Mercedes, TX 78570
(956) 565-0753

*Champion Boots
505 S Cotton
El Paso, TX 79901
(915) 534-7783

* Champion Attitude Boots
507 S Cotton
El Paso, TX 79901
(888) 547-7266

Chism Boots
403 E Tarrant
Llano, TX 78643
(325) 247-4258

Chris Bennett Boot Company
1152-2 N Hohokam Dr
Nogales, AZ 85621
(520) 287-6688

Circle C Boot Shop
106A S Old Betsey Road
Keene, TX 76059
(817) 641-4424

Cobbler Stone Boots
4311 Little Rd
Arlington, TX 76016
(817) 516-7551

Coe Custom Boots
PO Box 1674
Alturas, CA 96101
(530) 233-2564

Cool Hand Custom
7350 Old Gringo Hwy 54
Fulton, MO 65251
(573) 642-6918

Cottle's Boots
2803 Wolflin
Amarillo, TX 79109
(806) 352-8821

Crary Custom Boots & Shoes
8235 SE Stark St
Portland, OR 97216
(503) 253-8984

Country Cobbler
PO Box 151
Cody, WY 82414
(307) 527-7491

Cunningham's Lone Star Boots
4606 Mimosa Ln
Wichita Falls, TX 76310
(940) 781-4505

Custom Boots by Morado
402 Frisco St
Houston, TX 77022
(713) 694-7571

Custom Footwear, Inc.
835 E Southern Ave #1
Mesa, AZ 85204
(480) 461-1940

Daly Boots
7358 Reindeer Trail
San Antonio, TX 78238
(210) 682-6668

Dan Freeman Boots
2 Park Street
Middlebury, VT 05753
(802) 388-2515

Dave J. Hutchings Boots
8410 Garfield Way
Thornton, CO 80229
(303) 289-6726

*****David Espinosa Bootmaker**
6042 N 16th St
Phoenix, AZ 85016
(602) 263-8164

*****David Espinosa Bootmaker**
7236 E. 1st Ave
Scottsdale, AZ 85251
(480) 421-2166

*****David's Boots**
3441 W Sahara Ave, #D-5
Las Vegas, NV 89102
(702) 871-0350

*****David's Boots**
346 N Moreley Ave S
Nogales, AZ 85621
(800) 454-4842

*****Davis Custom Boots**
1209 E 11th St
Quanah, TX 79252
(940) 839-6537

*****Dean's Boot Shop**
710 N Turner
Hobbs, NM 88240
(505) 393-6583

Little's Boots.

Deeter Boots
PO Box 117
LaSal, UT 84530
(435) 686-2268

Don Atkinson Custom Boots
229 C Old Ingram Loop
Ingram, TX 78028
(830) 367-5400

**Dorward Custom
Cow-Boy Boots**
117 South 2nd
Guthrie, OK 73044
(405) 282-1258

Driftwood Custom Boots
2307 Central
Poteau, OK 74953
(918) 647-2085

Dubois Boots & Leather
183 W Main
Dubois, ID 83423
(208) 374-5490

Duck Menzies Bootmaker
1636 W FM 93
Temple, TX 76502
(254) 933-2485

 ## E

E. P. Martin Boot Shop
31277 Hwy 183
Las Animas, CO 81054
(719) 456-2938

El Paso Boots
1105 E Yandell
El Paso, TX 79902
(915) 533-8110

Little's Boots.

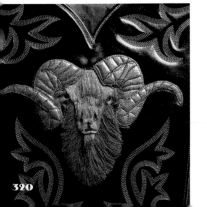

El Toro Boot Shop
7604 Acapulco Ave
El Paso, TX 79915
(915) 591-3508

F

*Falconhead (Tres Outlaws)
11911 San Vicente Blvd #150
Los Angeles, CA 90049
(310) 471-7075

Fit Well Boot & Saddle Company
Hwy 48 & 48A
Coleman, OK 73432
(580) 937-4676

Flint Boot & Hat Shop
3035-34th St
Lubbock, TX 79410
(806) 797-7060

Frank English Custom Boots
80085 Gallatin Rd
Bozeman, MT 59718
(406) 582-7467

G

Gary's Boots
PO Box 14903
Spokane, WA 99214
(509) 891-1756

 ## H

Harshman Boots
1712 Mohawk
Edmond, OK 73013
(405) 818-5507

Hickman Custom Boots
PO Box 1207
Chino Valley, AZ 86323
(520) 636-5461

Higdon Boots
5605 W 41st
Amarillo, TX 79109
(806) 353-3951

Huseby Custom Boots
7154B 4th
Bonners Ferry, ID 83805
(208) 267-2924

J

*J. B. Hill Boot Company
335 N Clark Dr
El Paso, TX 79905
(915) 599-1551

J. L. Mercer & Son Boots
224 South Chadbourne
San Angelo, TX 76903
(325) 658-7634

J.P.'s Custom Handmade Boots
106 E Hwy 54
Box 625
Camdenton, MO 65020
(573) 346-7711

Jackson's Boots
10733 Leopard
Corpus Christi, TX 78410
(361) 241-2628

Jake's Custom Boots & Saddles
1002 Sunset Valley Dr
Mountain View, AR 72560
(870) 585-2323

James Leddy Boot Company
1602 N Treadaway
Abilene, Texas 79601
(325) 677-7811

James Owens Boots
PO Box 776
Clarendon, TX 79226
(806) 874-9812

Jass Boot Shop (Pablo)
803 E Ave G
Lampasas, TX 76550
(512) 556-3857

Jass Boot Shop (John)
501 B South Key Ave
Lampasas, TX 76550
(512) 556-2729

Jim Covington Bootmaker
418 Parker St
Gardner, MA 01440
(978) 632-1869

Jim's Boot Shop
736 TJ King Road
Lockesburg, AR 71846
(870) 289-5231

Jimmy's Boot Shop
211 E Tyler St
Athens, TX 75751
(903) 675-5038

John Cessnun Boot Shop
405 Freida
Hot Springs, AR 71913
(501) 623-3069

Johnny Reb Boot Company
100 Landing Ln
Carson City, NV 89704
(775) 882-5900

Johnson Station Boot Company
2210 W Houston St
Broken Arrow, OK 74012
(918) 258-1809

Kimmel Boots
2080 CR 304
Comanche, TX 76442
(325) 356-3197

Klemmer Boot
PO Box 122
Salmon, ID 83467
(208) 756-6444

Kraig Jillson Bootmaker
3005 Center St
Anderson, CA 96007
(530) 378-2698

Lefty's Leathercraft
323-7 Otoyoshi-Cho
Masuda-Shimane
698-0003-Japan
(1-81) 856-22-8240

Len Boden Custom Boots
117 A CR 353
Merkel, TX 79536
(325) 928-5301

Leprechaun Boot Shop
224 N Main
Weatherford, TX 76086
(817) 594-5445

*Liberty Boot Company
224 Shaw St
Toronto, ON, Canada
(416) 588-5013

*Little's Boots
110 Division Ave
San Antonio, TX 78214
(210) 923-2221

Lonesome Ace Boot Company
3501-1/2 W Walsh Place
Denver, CO 80219
(303) 935-2584

Loveless Custom Boots
2434 SW 29th
Oklahoma City, OK 73119
(405) 631-9731

*Lucchese Boots
203 W Water St
Santa Fe, NM 87501
(800) 871-1883

MJN Boot & Leather Shop
27210-468th Ave
Tea, SD 57064
(605) 368-2922

*M.L. Leddy Boot & Saddlery
2200 Beauregard
San Angelo, TX 76901
(325) 942-7655

Madison Valley Custom Boots
14960 Homestead Rd
Riley, KS 66531
(785) 485-2772

*Maida's Black Jack Boot Company
3948 Westheimer
Houston, TX 77027
(713) 961-4538

Marshall's Boot Shop
7317 E 181st St S
Bixby, OK 74008
(918) 366-9880

Matt Newberry Custom Boots
46326 Lone Fir Rd
Halfway, OR 97834
(541) 742-4089

McGlasson Custom Boots
PO Box 14903
Spokane, WA 99206
(509) 891-1756

McGuffin Boots
1113 Nashville SW
Albuquerque, NM 87105
(505) 452-0690
Teaches bootmaking

Meanwhile Back at the Ranch/ Heather Joy
710 E 146th
Glenpool, OK 74033
(918) 322-9808

Melody's Custom Boots
446 W Kanai Ave
Porterville, CA 93257
(559) 782-8076

Mercedes Boot Company
2440 White Settlement Rd
Ft. Worth, TX 76107
(800) 552-2668

Merrell's Custom Boots/ Merrell Institute of Bootmaking
3400 N 3500 W
Vernal, UT 84078
(435) 789-3079

Michael Anthony Boots
227 N Main St
Sebastopol, CA 95472
(707) 823-7204

Mike DeWitt
1801 E 4th St
Okmulgee, OK 74447
(918) 293-5342
Teaches bootmaking

*Mingo Boot Company
6966 Alameda
El Paso, TX 79915
(915) 779-7681

*Montana Boots
201 S Bridge St
Henrietta, TX 76365
(940) 538-5691

Morado Boots
402 Frisco St
Houston, Texas 77022
(713) 694-7571

Myer Custom Boots
1241 W 25th
Houston, TX 77008
(713) 864-3808

★ **N** ★
*Nathalie
503 Canyon Rd
Santa Fe, NM 87501
(505) 982-1021

Vintage 1950s.

Nevin's Custom Boots
1456 W Marguarite
Willcox, AZ 85643
(520) 384-2941

No Name Boot Company
4213 N Starr Rd
Otis Orchards, WA 99027
(509) 226-1980

★ **O** ★
*Old Gringo
755 Emory St
Imperial Beach, CA 91932
(619) 575-2810

★ **P** ★
P. K. Bootmaker
600 Miller Valley
Prescott, AZ 86301
(928) 442-1213

Palace Boot Shop
1212 Prairie
Houston, TX 77002
(713) 224-1411

Pascal Boots
4738 Farmdale Ave
Studio City, CA 91602
(818) 506-4668

Paul Bond Boot Company
915 Paul Bond Dr
Nogales, AZ 85621
(520) 281-0512

Pound's Custom Boots
PO Box 68
Corona, NM 88318
(505) 849-7744

**Richard O. Cook Custom
Boots**
56 E Nunez
Stonewall, TX 78671
(830) 644-2760

**Frank's Boot
Shop, 1940–50.**

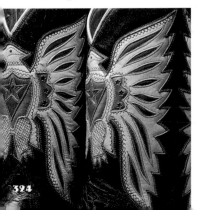

Rocketbuster Boots
115 S Anthony
El Paso, TX 79901
(915) 541-1300

Rod Patrick Bootmakers
PO Box 1719
Weatherford, TX 76086
(817) 596-7026

Ron's Custom Boots
317 E Cotton St
Longview, TX 75601
(903) 753-4600

Roper Boot Shop
1421 Broadway
Kerrville, TX 78028
(830) 257-3911

Runnin' Hare Boot Shop
12505 Old Mill Creek Rd
Brenham, TX 77833
(979) 289-9301

Rusty Franklin Boot Co.
3275 Arden Rd
San Angelo, TX 76901
(325) 653-2668

Ryan's Custom Boots
431 N Last Chance Gulch
Helena, MT 59061
(406) 442-5215

S. D. Brookshire Boots
4302 US Hwy 81 N
Bowie, TX 76230
(940) 872-4720

Saunders Custom Boots
311 G St
Central City, NE 68826
(308) 946-3879

Sierra Boots
1529 E Paisano Dr
El Paso, TX 79901
(915) 873-3933

Slickfork Boots
558 Printz Rd
Arroyo Grande, CA 93420
(805) 481-4944

Sorrell Custom Boots
306 W Industrial
Guthrie, OK 73044
(405) 282-5464

Spikes Custom Boots
1202 E Spring
Henrietta, TX 76365
(940) 538-4864

Stephanie Ferguson
Custom Boots
2112 Poe Prairie Rd
Millsap, TX 76066
(817) 341-9700

Stewarts Custom
Boots
30 W 28th St
S. Tucson, AZ 85713
(520) 622-2706

Stockman Boots
106 S Chicago
Hot Springs, SD 57747
(605) 745-6771

★ **T** ★

T. J. Hall Boot Company
4160 Duranzo
El Paso, TX 79905
(877) 730-1118

Tlo Lowry
30-B Steel Dust
Moriarty, NM 87035
(505) 832-5370

*T. O. Stanley Boots
4610 Duranzo
El Paso, TX 79905
(877) 730-1118

Taylor Boots
224 N Main
Weatherford, TX 76086
(817)594-5445

Taylor Made Boots
1007 E Williams St
Breckenridge, TX 76424
(254) 559-1861

Tex Robin Boots
115 W 8th St
Coleman, TX 76834
(325) 625-5556

Texas Custom Boots
2525 S Lamar Blvd
Austin, TX 78704
(512) 442-0926

Texas Traditions
2222 College Ave
Austin, TX 78704
(512) 443-4447

Three-R Custom Boots
PO Box 521
Checotah, OK 74426
(918) 759-8280

Tom Smith Custom Boots
PO Box 482
Aspermont, TX 79502
(940) 989-3385

Trail Town Custom Boots
107 S Broad
Saint Jo, TX 76265
(940) 841-2285

Tres Outlaws Boot Company
421 S Cotton St
El Paso, TX 79901
(915) 544-2727

Ty Skiver
5535 Janine Way
Corning, CA 96021
(530) 824-0443

★ ★

Valley Boots
280 N Moapa Valley Blvd
Overton, NV 89040

★ ★

Western Leather
Craft Boot Shop
1950 Civic Circle
Amarillo, TX 79109
(806) 355-0174

Western Leather Craft Boots
305 Ave H NW
Childress, TX 79201
(940) 937-2788

Wheeler Boot Company
4115 Willowbend
Houston, TX 77025
(713) 665-0224

*Wilson Boots
955 Penny Dr
Ashland, OR 97520
(541) 951-0952

Wild Bill's Boots
20 Lakeside Dr
Granby, CT 06035
(860) 844-8440

William Shanor and Julie Bonney
955 Penny Dr
Ashland, OR 97520
(541) 552-0219

Woodward Custom Boots
25077 Veijas Blvd
Descanso, CA 91916
(619) 659-5040

Ye Olde Leather Boot
Worth St
Hemphill, TX 75948
(409) 787-1233

Yiorgos Boots
5 Dorval Rod
Toronto, ON, Canada M6P-2B2
(416) 530-4597

Young's Custom Boots
808 Backus
Paducah, TX 79248
(806) 492-3103

Vintage 1950–60.

Jennifer June's Cowboy Boot Web Page is the definitive web resource on cowboy boots. Established in 1997, **www.dimlights.com** now welcomes more than 34,000 visitors each month, providing information and entertainment to a growing online community of folks who make, wear, and admire cowboy boots. Don't miss Jennifer's state-by-state list of custom bootmakers, her regional map of Texas bootmakers, or the photo essays of her field trips to some of America's best-loved boot shops.

The Museums with the Booty

**Autry Museum of
Western Heritage**
4700 Western Heritage Way
Los Angeles, CA 90027
(323) 667-2000

**The Bob Bullock Texas
State History Museum**
1800 N Congress Ave
Austin, TX 78711
(512) 936-8746

Buffalo Bill Historical Center
720 Sheridan Ave
Cody, WY 82414
(307) 587-4771

Country Music Hall of Fame
222 Fifth Ave S
Nashville, TN 37203
(800) 852-6437

Gilcrease Museum
1400 N Gilcrease Museum Rd
Tulsa, OK 74127
(918) 596-2700

**National Cowboy and
Western Heritage Museum**
1700 NE 63rd St
Oklahoma City, OK 73111
(405) 478-2250

**National Cowgirl Museum
and Hall of Fame**
1720 Gendy St
Fort Worth, TX 76107
(817) 336-4475

Opryland USA Museum
2800 Opryland Dr
Nashville, TN 37214
(615) 889-1000

**Panhandle-Plains
Historical Museum**
2401-4th Ave
Canyon, TX 79016
(806) 656-2244

**Roy Rogers &
Dale Evans Museum**
3950 Green Mountain
Branson, Missouri
(417) 339-1900

**Smithsonian Institute
National Mall**
14th St and Constitution Ave
Washington, DC 20560
(202) 357-2700

**Texas Ranger Hall of
Fame and Museum**
I-35, Exit 335B
PO Box 2570
Waco, TX 78702
(254) 750-8631

Tom Mix Museum
721 N Delaware
Dewey, OK 74029
(918) 534-1555

Witte Museum
3801 Broadway
San Antonio, TX 78209
(210) 357-1900

The Current Crop of Vintage Boot Dealers

Back at the Ranch
209 E Marcy St
Santa Fe, NM 87501
(888) 96BOOTS

Blackmail
1202 S Congress Ave
Austin, TX 78704
(512) 326-7670

Butch Brown
Call for appointment
(254) 865-8999

Sharon & Bryant Dalby
Call for appointment
(210) 326-5616
(210) 710-8034

Double Take at the Ranch
319 S Guadalupe St
Santa Fe, NM 87501
(505) 820-7775

Hopalong Boot Company
3908 Rodeo Rd
Santa Fe, NM 87501
(505) 471-5570

Horsefeathers
109 B Kit Carson Rd
Taos, NM 87571
(505) 758-7457

Iron Jack's
PO Box 71
Claremont, CA 91711
(909) 624-5656

J & S Old Western Store & Museum
Rt. 1, Box 315-C
Warsaw, MO 65355
(660) 438-2631

Katy K's
2407 12th Ave S
Nashville, TN 37204
(615) 297-4242

Kowboyz
8050 Beverly Blvd
Los Angeles, CA 90048
(323) 653-6444

Nathalie
503 Canyon Rd
Santa Fe, NM 87501
(505) 982-1021

Sasse
Call for appointment
(505) 983-1944

Ugly
5322 College Ave
Oakland, CA 94618
(510) 420-1740